THE GLOBALIZATION BACKLASH

———

Colin Crouch

T0056364

polity

Copyright © Colin Crouch 2019

The right of Colin Crouch to be identified as Author of this Work has been asserted in accordance with the UK Copyright, Designs and Patents Act 1988.

First published in 2019 by Polity Press
Reprinted 2019

Polity Press
65 Bridge Street
Cambridge CB2 1UR, UK

Polity Press
101 Station Landing
Suite 300
Medford, MA 02155, USA

All rights reserved. Except for the quotation of short passages for the purpose of criticism and review, no part of this publication may be reproduced, stored in a retrieval system or transmitted, in any form or by any means, electronic, mechanical, photocopying, recording or otherwise, without the prior permission of the publisher.

ISBN-13: 978-1-5095-3376-3
ISBN-13: 978-1-5095-3377-0 (pb)

A catalogue record for this book is available from the British Library.

Library of Congress Cataloging-in-Publication Data

Names: Crouch, Colin, 1944- author.
Title: The globalization backlash / Colin Crouch.
Description: Cambridge, UK ; Medford, MA : Polity, 2018. | Includes
   bibliographical references and index.
Identifiers: LCCN 2018019540 (print) | LCCN 2018028944 (ebook) | ISBN
   9781509533794 (Epub) | ISBN 9781509533763 (hardback) | ISBN 9781509533770
   (pbk.)
Subjects: LCSH: Globalization--Public opinion. | Globalization--Economic
   aspects. | Economic policy. | International economic relations.
Classification: LCC HF1365 (ebook) | LCC HF1365 .C78 2018 (print) | DDC
   303.48/2--dc23
LC record available at https://lccn.loc.gov/2018019540

Typeset in 11 on 14 pt Sabon by
Servis Filmsetting Ltd, Stockport, Cheshire
Printed and bound in the United States by LSC Communications.

The publisher has used its best endeavours to ensure that the URLs for external websites referred to in this book are correct and active at the time of going to press. However, the publisher has no responsibility for the websites and can make no guarantee that a site will remain live or that the content is or will remain appropriate.

Every effort has been made to trace all copyright holders, but if any have been overlooked the publisher will be pleased to include any necessary credits in any subsequent reprint or edition.

For further information on Polity, visit our website: politybooks.com

For Joan

Contents

1 The Issues   *page* 1

2 The Economy   13

3 Culture and Politics   49

4 The Future   84

Notes   114

1

The Issues

An epic struggle between globalization and a resurgent nationalism is changing political identities and conflicts across the world. While the term 'globalization' refers primarily to the development of relatively unrestricted economic relationships across most of the world, that process has wider social and political implications. People from diverse cultures are drawn together, and national systems of economic governance are challenged. Various kinds of upheaval – economic, cultural and political – accompany globalization, producing a backlash among those who feel negatively affected. From being a process that seemed simply to be bringing us both cheaper products from abroad and new export opportunities, globalization has come for many to mean the loss, not just of individual jobs, but of entire long-established industries and the communities and ways of life associated with them, spiralling into further disorientation as foreign customs and large numbers of persons from other cultures invade and obscure life's familiar landmarks. The consequent unease is felt alike by American and French former steel workers who have seen their industries and local communities disappear; by Germans talking about *Heimat* and feeling that it represents something they have lost; by Russians, British and Austrians nostalgic for lost empires and resenting the fact that, in a globalizing world, 'sovereignty' has to be shared; by people in Islamic societies feeling invaded by American and British warplanes as well as by western cultures and sexual mores; and by people across Europe and North America horrified by occasional acts of Islamic terrorism and disliking the presence in their streets of women wearing the *hijab*.

Globalization threatens some people's desire to feel pride in the circumstances of their lives – in their work, their cultural identity, their communities, the towns and cities where they live, that broad bundle of ideas implied in the German idea of *Heimat*. Many people are still able to feel this pride, as the areas in which they live and the sectors in which they work have been favoured by globalization; they have relaxed, optimistic and even eager approaches to the opportunities presented by the kaleidoscope of an ever more varied cultural universe. But others have a different experience. Even if they are prosperous in their own lives, they see a wider world of bewildering change, and yearn for the certainties that they, perhaps mistakenly, believe characterized an earlier one.

During the prolonged discussion that took place in the United Kingdom (UK) after the 2016 referendum on leaving the European Union (EU) (the so-called 'Brexit'), the British Broadcasting Corporation (BBC) interviewed some people in Middlesbrough, a very depressed, former industrial city in the north-east of England that had voted heavily to leave the EU. A recurrent theme of the interviews was: we have lost everything; our young people leave to go elsewhere; we see no prospects for our future; but at least we know that we are British, and we feel pride in that. Therefore, they voted to leave the EU. There is no logic in the strict sense in that chain of argument, but there is a powerful emotional logic. It helps explain why a resurgent nationalism is becoming a dominant popular force in the early twenty-first century.

But the lack of strict logic has to be contested. We can only gain a measure of control over a world of increasing interdependence by growing identities, as well as institutions of democracy and governance, that can themselves reach beyond the nation state. This task is hard enough in itself; it becomes virtually impossible when large numbers of politicians, newspapers and intellectuals are telling people to do exactly the opposite and seal themselves behind national barriers, treating immigrants as a disease that pollutes their culture, relating to the rest of the world only through arm's-length trade – and therefore leaving transnational corporations and deregulated financial markets beyond control.

Although opposition to globalization comes from all recognizable parts of the political spectrum, its leadership has been firmly in the hands of the traditionalist, nationalistic right. This is interesting. Economic globalization is mainly a project of neoliberalism, which for several decades has been the dominant ideology of the modern right. Does this mean that politics has become a fight between different factions of the right, and that the left no longer has meaning? Or do differences between left and right have no relevance in the struggle over globalization? I shall argue here that left and right certainly retain meaning; that the social democratic left has

3

a distinct contribution to make to this conflict; that it needs to stand on the side of globalization against the new nationalism; but that it must also insist on reforms to the shape that the process is taking. This in no way means – indeed, must not mean – abandoning national and more local identities. Rather, the multiple identities available to us in today's world become a series of concentric circles, enriching each other and rooted in a cooperative subsidiarity – or a Russian *matryoshka* doll, with successive dolls of different sizes nested comfortably within each other. We need to be proud of our town or city, of the region within which it is located, of the country within which that is contained, of European institutions (for those fortunate enough to live in a country that is a member of the EU) and of wider global entities. This is only possible if constructive developments are occurring at each of these levels, and where their creative mutual interdependence is clear. We need political and social leaders who are willing to work at reinforcing the links across these levels, helping them to work positively together, leaders who cease insisting on absurd rivalries and an outdated search for sovereignty in a world where no individual person, region or country can stand alone without deep cooperation with others.

Behind all these issues stands a new stage in the great conflict, dating back to the eighteenth century, between the values of the *ancien régime* and those of the Enlightenment: between the security of conservative authority and familiar tradition on the one hand, and the freedom of rationality, innovation and change on the other. If globalization is examined in these, rather than economic, terms, it is easy to understand hostility to it on the traditionalist, nationalist, but not neoliberal, right. Perhaps it is because in recent decades we have become so accustomed to regarding neoliberalism as the principal force on the right that left-wing opponents of globalization have been rather unaware of the reactionary company they are keeping. The leftist argument against globalization is understandable enough in its own terms. Broadly, it runs as follows:

1. Globalization has involved the extension of capitalism over ever more parts of the world, achieved by breaking down those regulatory barriers that enabled national governments to ensure that firms and markets adhered to certain norms. In other words, globalization allows capitalism to destroy the governance mechanisms that contained those excesses that cause poverty, inequality and the neglect of collective needs.
2. The highest level of governance at which democracy has become established is the nation state. Therefore, as soon as a phenomenon escapes that level, it escapes the reach of democracy and falls under the sole control of the capitalist elites that dominate transnational space.
3. The nation state is not only a democratic level in a formal sense, but also an entity with which most ordinary working people identify; they are willing to commit themselves to it. That kind of commitment will be necessary if democratic political power is to contest the domination of deregulated capitalism.
4. The welfare state, in particular, has been a national construction, drawing on the solidarity with one another that members of a nation feel, members of

a shared community, as captured in the Swedish concept of the welfare state as a *folkshem* (people's home, 'home' here meaning, like the German *Heimat*, a place where one feels 'at home').

5. It is indeed notable that the strongest welfare states developed in the Nordic countries at a time when these were ethnically and culturally highly homogeneous, and that their fragmentation in recent years has been associated with the arrival of large numbers of immigrants and asylum seekers, mainly from Islamic cultures. It is also notable that the ethnically heterogeneous society of the United States of America (USA) has one of the weakest and least generous welfare states in the democratic world. There seems to be a trade-off between a strong welfare state and liberal multiculturalism; if so, the left had better abandon the latter as fast as it can. (This, it should be noted, is a far more respectable argument than one simply telling left-wing parties to run after the xenophobic right in the search for votes.)

6. Globalization and multiculturalism being inimical to a social democratic project, there needs to be a turn towards economic protection and controls over capital movements, and severe restrictions on immigration. For European countries, this means at least a severe limit to, if not total withdrawal from, the process of European integration – which especially in recent years has meant integration on neoliberal terms.

Each step in the progression of this argument is logical, but at point 5 it starts to lead to the path of the xenophobic right, even if for different reasons. We can find examples of where precisely this is happening. Among political parties, there is the position of the French leftist party France Insoumise (literally, France 'Unsubmitted'), and of the now-dominant left of the British Labour Party. Both, though particularly the former, are inclined towards protectionist economic positions; both are hostile to the EU; and both have ambiguous positions on immigration. Neither shares the outright hostility to immigrants and ethnic minorities of the far right, but they move away from liberal approaches to the issue. France Insoumise rejects an obligation on France to take a share of asylum seekers from North Africa and the Middle East arriving on the shores of Greece and Italy, but stops short of attacking the refugees themselves. The Labour Party never criticizes ethnic minorities originating in countries of the British Commonwealth; these people have the vote, and tend to vote Labour. It has, however, echoed general criticisms of immigrants from EU countries (who do not have the vote), concentrating on their possible negative impact on wage levels and working conditions. The Danish Social Democratic Party currently finds itself part of a triangle comprising: itself as the main opposition party; a minority government of a neoliberal, pro-globalization party trying to weaken the welfare state; and a far-right, xenophobic but pro-welfare party maintaining the neoliberals in office. The social democrats are divided over a strong temptation to forge a pro-welfare alliance with the far right, against the neoliberals. More difficult to place on the left–right spectrum is the Italian party Movimento Cinque Stelle (M5S, Five Star Movement), now the largest party in the country. Founded by a comedian, Beppe Grillo, noted for his scathing criticisms of corruption in the Italian political and business elite, it attracted many supporters from the left. It makes policy through crowd-sourcing. This led it to discover considerable hostility among Italians to the refugees arriving on their southern shores; as a result, this issue became prominent on its policy platform, and attracted votes. The party now finds itself in government with the anti-immigrant party La Lega, committed to building internment camps for refugees and to other anti-Islamic measures.

Among academic commentators, the German sociologist and political scientist Wolfgang Streeck has pointed to the basis of the welfare state in national solidarity, and for that reason opposes the EU,[1] but has never criticized ethnic minorities or immigrants. David Goodhart, a prominent British journalist and social commentator, on the other hand, has explicitly blamed the cultural dilution of Britain caused by immigration for weakening support for the welfare state.[2] He, too, does not attack immigrants or people from ethnic and cultural minorities themselves, but those liberal members of the host society who have not appreciated that welfare states have been national and even ethnic in their appeal to solidarity, and that there is difficulty in enabling them to transcend that level. Therefore, it seems to follow, developments that diminish the sovereignty of the national political level must be resisted, and national societies must restrict their ethnic heterogeneity. The problem with this kind of reasoning, sociologically sound though it is in many respects, is that it leads to a conservative resistance to any kind of change that tries to move democratic politics and feelings of human solidarity beyond the nation state, which then remains frozen in time.

Such positions necessarily oppose globalization. Given

the strength of the economic pressure for globalization and the extent to which it has progressed, trying to reverse it now would require multiple allies, and appeals to strong feelings and beliefs that would bring popular support to bear to confront the economic and corporate weight supporting globalization. Once that point has been reached, there becomes little to prevent left-wing critics of globalization from sharing the language and eventually the strategies of the far right.

Political groups on the right have a different dilemma. Over the years, the highly successful alliance of conservatism and neoliberalism has seen the former providing a base of traditional, nationally oriented stability with broad popular appeal, while the latter explores the entrepreneurial possibilities of a destabilizing global deregulation. The tensions inherent in that alliance are being stretched to breaking point as some conservatives respond to the decline of their past popular supports by increasing their reliance on nationalist sentiment. While the potential explosion of these tensions offers scope for optimism to the left, there is a cynical resolution of the right's dilemma that should alarm them. If concern at the disruption to life caused by neoliberalism can be channelled into blaming ethnic minorities and other potentially unpopular groups, strengthening the increasing xenophobia of conservatism, then neoliberals can be left in peace to intensify a globalizing insecurity that will then be blamed further on the minorities, reinforcing even further the appeal of their incongruous conservative allies.

This fairly accurately describes what has taken place in the UK and the USA since 2016. The decision of a majority of voters in the UK's referendum to leave the EU, a vote motivated strongly by a desire (in the words of a central 'Leave' slogan) to 'take back control', is being interpreted by its main champions as an opportunity to weaken labour rights and food hygiene laws. A weakening of labour rights is usually coded as advocacy of Britain outside the EU as 'the Singapore of the Atlantic', Singapore being a non-democratic state that manages to be a low-cost competitor by having few labour rights and a weak welfare state. Food hygiene is an issue as the UK seeks a trade deal with the USA as the main pillar of its post-EU trading relationships. On a visit to London on 6 November 2017, the US Commerce Secretary, Wilbur Ross, warned the UK that it would have to adopt the USA's (weaker) rules on food imports hygiene if it wanted such a deal. 'Control' is retrieved only to be thrown away. Donald Trump, elected President of the USA partly by relatively low-income voters feeling betrayed by the US elite, which he depicted as favouring ethnic minorities above white Americans, is himself a billionaire and rapidly set about trying to abolish public health care support and (more successfully) making major tax cuts for very rich individuals and corporations.

There is, however, also danger in the position to which my argument tends: for moderate forces of left and right to stand together for a regulated globalization against xenophobic forces. In practice, this entails the 'grand coalitions' of Christian and social democrats that governed Austria and Germany for several years until 2017, when they collapsed under the force – especially in the former country – of a resurgent xenophobia. Such coalitions provide in general good government, but they have two related negative consequences. First, they stifle political controversy between the centre right and centre left, generating a vast but soggy technocratic centre, forcing anyone wanting to contest it to the margins of extreme left and right. Second, they prevent the centre left in particular from recovering from the excessively uncritical stands towards unregulated globalization that had been taken by Third Way social democrats in the 1990s, and developing the credible new positions needed to remedy globalization's defects. This again drives voters to extremes offering anti-globalization policies.

I am here mainly concerned with the problems facing the centre left, and with the difficult task of trying to extend the reach of democracy, regulation and social policy to levels beyond the nation state. Only in that way might globalization serve human needs. I am writing for the concerned general reader; those seeking a more thoroughly detailed account of, say, the economics of globalization will need to turn to the several economic analyses available. A major aim here is to bring the economic issues at stake alongside the cultural and social questions raised by globalization. These two facets are usually treated separately, although the links between them are often recognized.

I emphatically reject the assertion of Goodhart and others that there is a direct choice between cosmopolitan and internationalist values and those that are rooted in local communities. To live in the twenty-first century means precisely to manage multiple identities, ranging from being rooted in a community to reaching out to transnational levels. Some political traditions of left and right alike find it difficult to embrace such a range. Others are more at ease with the principle of

11

subsidiarity, which seeks to have decisions and policy choices made at the most local level possible, subject to moving to higher levels when there is overall gain to be made by so doing. What that means in practice we shall explore below. We must first understand the nature of the backlash against globalization in its economic, cultural and political ramifications.

2

The Economy

It is difficult to draw up a balance sheet of gains and losses from globalization. Many variables need to enter the calculations, while different individuals vary in their estimation of the relative importance of, say, having fresh air to breathe and having the money to buy some decent clothes and furniture. Nevertheless, several observers have tried to make some overall assessments, ranging from official international bodies like the International Monetary Fund (IMF)[1] to individual economists, including François Bourguignon,[2] Branco Milanovic,[3] Dani Rodrik[4] and Joseph Stiglitz.[5] It is notable that these economists have in the past been senior staff members of the IMF or World Bank. While these organizations have themselves come to see negative aspects of globalization since the financial crisis of 2008, Rodrik and Stiglitz were sounding warnings at an earlier point. Readers wanting a fully detailed account should read their books. Here we can give just an overview, starting with a look at how globalization has developed, going on to assess its gains and losses, and finally considering its implications for economic sovereignty.

The waves of globalization

We can identify four waves of modern economic globalization.

The first wave: European imperialism

First came the extension of world trade in the late nineteenth century – a globalization episode often forgotten in recent accounts.[6] This was highly controlled by the western European empires – of Great Britain in particular, but also of France, the Netherlands, Belgium, Portugal and others. Being imperial, it was military as well as commercial, and eventually included 'the scramble for Africa', which in turn became one of the causes of the First World War.

However, the growth of industrial production in the period made possible a general increase in trade among many nations, including those, like the USA, not involved in the construction of overseas empires. There is no space here to describe the patterns and forms of governance involved, but the absence of any regulatory regime apart from those imposed by dominant countries was notable. In 1859, Japan was forced to accept trade with the USA under the threat of military invasion if it refused. Twice in the nineteenth century the UK used military action to persuade China to buy opium from British suppliers. Britain also controlled closely which goods it would allow its colonies to produce, to prevent competition with its own industries. Britain's self-proclaimed commitment to 'free' trade can be questioned. But international trade, which in past centuries was largely limited to exotic and expensive products, now began to involve those for ordinary working people, improving the lives of many, whether as consumers of cheap imported goods or as the producers of increased quantities of exports.

The years between the two world wars saw a major retreat from international trade, a rise of protectionism, the defeat of attempts through the League of Nations at broad international collaboration, and the rise of militarized, violent nationalism, particularly for Nazi Germany and its Italian and Japanese allies. These finally became major causes of the Second World War.

The second wave: US-dominated tariff reduction and European integration

Nationalism and insistence on uncompromising national sovereignty having become associated with Nazism and fascism, after the second World War politicians of most kinds in the western world moved firmly away from their slogans and passions, and set about constructing an architecture of international institutions. International trade recovered, but was no longer based on the European colonial empires. These were gradually disintegrating, being replaced by the global dominance of the USA. Thus began a second wave of globalization. The initial framework for a new system of rules for international economic relations was established at a key conference in Bretton Woods, New Hampshire, in 1944, though the USSR and its allies subsequently departed from the regime. The division of most of the world into the blocs of the Cold War limited the extent of the new system, as that dominated by the Soviet Union, and also that of China, remained outside the international market economy. But in the US-dominated part of the world, trade barriers were gradually relaxed in successive rounds of the General Agreement on Tariffs and Trade (GATT). There were no reasons for inhabitants of western countries to see the growth of international governance of trade as a challenge to their national 'sovereignty'; their interests dominated the whole process, and their governments' control over movements of capital and labour were left untouched. The exception of capital movements was important, as it enabled governments to avoid threats of capital flight if they constructed strongly redistributive taxation systems or strong demand management policies.

Among the countries that in 1957 formed the European Economic Community (EEC, later the EU), cross-national economic integration went further. Although the architects of European unity seriously envisaged, in the words of the Treaty of Rome, 'an ever-closer union' among member states, priority was given to trade. Individual countries were left to develop their own welfare states. These were seen as important to regaining legitimacy for governments in countries that had been fascist, or defeated and occupied during the war. On the other hand, social policy aims were never far from the European project: the EEC's origins lay in the Common Agricultural Policy and the European Coal and Steel Community, both designed to rescue and stabilize industries likely to be sources of social unrest if nothing was done to support them.

Meanwhile, the most fundamental symbol of national sovereignty – the power to wage war autonomously – had in reality been fundamentally compromised by the arrival of nuclear weapons, but this was not experienced as a problem except by a few who held nostalgically to old visions of empire. The European powers gradually abandoned their futile wars to prevent colonial independence, and, albeit beneath the terrifying anxiety of possible nuclear war, many parts of the world, and Europe in particular, became more peaceful than for many years.

There was one exception to the ease with which this limited globalization was accepted: growing immigration into several western economies brought episodes of violence, and more widespread discrimination and social rejection of immigrants. This happened both in countries where immigrants came mainly from former colonies, as in the UK, France, Belgium and the Netherlands, and in those to which they came as *Gastarbeiter* (guest workers), who, it was assumed, would go home after a period of years: Austria, Germany, Switzerland. The USA continued its far longer tradition of accepting immigration from across the world – with a similarly familiar story of accompanying ethnic conflict and discrimination. Political and economic elites often responded to anti-immigrant movements by imposing restrictions on the scale of future immigration, but they resisted temptations to increase their own support by exacerbating tensions. They still remembered what the encouragement of racial antagonism had caused in Germany in the 1930s. Racist and xenophobic organizations and politicians themselves were marginalized, and governments and civil society gradually developed ways of teaching native populations to accept the new people, whose labour was needed by economies in full expansion. Immigrant cultures, especially in food and music, enriched and were absorbed into host societies. Immigrants and natives began to form friendships and to intermarry.

The third wave: neoliberal deregulation

The expansion of world trade and agreements to reduce tariffs and other barriers moved to a new level during the 1980s in what we can see as a third wave of globalization, as it had different roots from the initial post-1945 desire to transcend nationalism. This was the general push for both domestic and international deregulation, as neoliberal economic ideas achieved dominance under the leadership of the USA and the UK. For neoliberals, the most important institution in governing human affairs is the market. There is a role for law in sustaining the property rights and trading obligations necessary for the market to function efficiently, but neoliberals are indifferent, even hostile, to ideas of nation. If markets are to be free and sovereign, there is no place for governments to defend a national economic interest against them; national and even transnational regulatory regimes are seen only as protectionism. The public power should be immune to popular pressures. This condition is found more easily at the international than the national level, as democratic politics is far livelier at the latter.

Under the impact of these two waves of globalization, mass production in steel, shipbuilding and several metalworking and electronics industries in Europe and North America became uncompetitive in the face of lower-cost competition. There was growing unemployment in many old industrial areas in wealthy countries, though within the EEC this was alleviated by structural funds to help regeneration. Those parts of the affected sectors that remained moved into specialized, high-value-added products, but employed far fewer people. Employment in services sectors, especially public services, grew at the same time. These, many of which needed to be delivered

18

close to the customer or user, were less vulnerable to international competition. In general, growth of this new employment outweighed the losses of jobs in manufacturing and mining.

A further important element of this period of globalization was the beginning of a deregulation of financial movements. The main negative consequences of this were to follow during the fourth wave, when they were coupled with the relaxation of banking rules, generating the crisis of 2007–8. The main consequence of the initial deregulation was to remove the safeguards of Bretton Woods over national control of capital movements, making it difficult for governments to pursue policies that conflicted with the interests of major capital holders. While countries remained free to opt out of the new system, to do so would cut off themselves and firms located in their jurisdictions from access to international funds, and encourage capital flight. However, for advanced economies (the issue is not so benign in developing countries), there is evidence that, provided governments manage their deficits effectively and constrain inflation, holders of global capital take little interest in the details of domestic policy; whether or not to have strong welfare states remains the choice of national electorates.[7]

Finally, institutions of cross-national economic governance providing more compliance with free trading norms – in exchange for lower tariffs and mutual acceptance of product standards – than was being achieved through GATT were erected at the level of specific world regions: for example, ASEAN in South-East Asia, Mercosur in South America, NAFTA in North America – but, most fully and successfully, the EEC.

*The fourth wave: the European Single Market, the
collapse of communism and the rise of the Far East*
These processes were massively reinforced by various
new developments in the 1990s, the combined impact
of which has been so great that it amounts to a fourth
wave of globalization.

- In 1995, the GATT was replaced by the World Trade
  Organization (WTO). Countries in membership of
  the WTO can trade in goods with each other without
  high tariff walls, provided they abide by certain rules.
  These mainly concern undertaking not to use protectionism or state subsidies of industries. This has
  served as a major incentive to governments to limit
  state intervention in the economy and to shape their
  trade policies in conformity with WTO rules.
- With particular enthusiasm on the part of the UK, the
  EU began to construct the European Single Market
  (ESM), which established common standards for
  unrestrained trade across a variety of goods, services
  and financial flows, and the free movement of labour,
  with a supranational court, the European Court of
  Justice (ECJ), to govern its implementation.
- At about the same time, the collapse of the Soviet
  Empire enabled Russia and the countries of central
  and eastern Europe to join the market economy, with
  those in central Europe eventually becoming full
  members of the EU – again with especially strong
  support from the UK.
- China, while formally maintaining its position as a
  state-socialist economy, also entered the market economy, joining the WTO in 2001. (Russia followed in
  2012.)

- The Multi-Fibre Arrangement, which had been established in 1974 to protect the world's wealthy economies from cheap clothing and textile imports from developing countries, especially in Asia, expired in 2004. This put heavy pressure on mass-market clothing and textile production, especially in southern Europe.
- The USA and UK had started deregulating the global financial system in the 1980s. This spread to other parts of the world in the 1990s. It funded major expansions of economic activity, but at the same time encouraged the irresponsible financial practices that by 2008 brought much of the world to a massive financial crisis.

Globalization was now in full spate, and in many respects followed the classic expectations of economists that there would be mutual gains from an expansion of free trade. Low-valued-added activities declined in the rich countries, to be replaced by both higher-value-added ones and activities in services that could not easily be replaced by imports, such as health, education, restaurants and retail trading. Firms in many poor countries, particularly China and the Indian subcontinent, began to dominate traditional manufacturing and mining activities, thereby increasing their national incomes. As a result, these countries developed a large middle class that could afford to buy expensive goods from Europe, Japan and the USA. The expansion of international trade began to be a positive-sum game. This is often obscured by politicians and business people who talk in terms of a 'global race', in which their countries must participate, with a strong sense that there

21

must be winners and losers. They do this in order to encourage workers to accept limited wage rises and cuts in public spending in order to boost 'competitiveness'. They forget (or conceal) that competitiveness can mean moving up-market to high-skilled, high-infrastructure activities, and not just keeping prices (and therefore wages and social costs) low. But another consequence was the financial crisis. This eventually contributed heavily to the wave of disillusion with the whole globalization process, and some modicum of realization among policy-makers that the deregulation of finance had gone too far and might threaten the globalization project itself. As Paul Mason, a British left-wing economics commentator, put it, 'if we want to save globalization, we have to ditch neoliberalism'.[8]

Globalization also brought increased migration, especially as multinational firms recruit their employees across the world. This process becomes cumulative, as certain regions acquire a reputation for a welcoming cosmopolitanism, leading them to attract more immigrants. Cities like London, Paris, New York and several in California have become highly multilingual and multicultural. Even low-paid jobs in rich countries have been attractive to people living in poor countries. Entry from abroad into the labour market, unlike into those for capital and products, is usually tightly controlled by governments, but the EU long ago established the principle of free movement for citizens of its member states. Free movement became problematic after the admission of the countries of Central and Eastern Europe (CEE), whose standard of living in the protectionist economies of the state-socialist period had fallen far behind that of the majority of western Europeans. This led to far greater numbers of migrants than had been envisaged when the principle of free movement had been established. Most western member states took measures to delay the extension of the free movement right for several years after countries were admitted to the Union, in the expectation that an improvement would take place in eastern economies, reducing immigration flows. The UK, Ireland and Sweden did not take advantage of this possibility, and therefore experienced a large initial wave of immigration until the rest of western Europe opened its borders. For nearly all western European countries except the UK immigration from CEE has ceased to be controversial, but considerable conflict has been aroused by a quite different phenomenon: waves of refugees and asylum seekers escaping from wars and other disasters in the Middle East and North Africa. Although not a direct consequence of the reduction of barriers to trade, this phenomenon has several links to globalization in general, and is certainly responsible for some of the opposition to it.

Gains and losses from globalization

We must now put some flesh on these generalizations with some key examples, focusing mainly on the world's most populous country, China, on which much western anxiety over globalization has concentrated. (Unless otherwise stated, the following data are taken from the World Bank's most recent *World Development Indicators*.[9]) The overall wealth of the Chinese people has certainly increased. In 1990, gross national income per capita in purchasing power parities stood at $US990 (in the USA, it was $23,730). By 2016, it had become $15,500 (the US equivalent was then $58,030). In 1990, exports represented 14% of China's gross domestic product (GDP); by 2016, this had risen to 20% of the far larger economy. (The comparable figures for the USA are 9% and 13%.) But China also increased its imports from the rest of the world, from 11% to 17% of GDP. (The USA's figure increased from the same 1990 level as China's to only 15%.) China's advance has therefore involved not only exports, but also imports from the rest of the world.

China's growing wealth has, however, been increasingly unequally divided. The World Institute for Development Economics Research of the United Nations University (UNU-WIDER) has calculated Gini coefficient measures of inequality for most countries.[10] The China of the Communist Cultural Revolution was very poor and the regime brutal, but relatively egalitarian, with a Gini coefficient of around 0.30 (broadly similar to the Nordic and certain central European countries). With China's entry into the global economy, inequality rose steeply: by 2015, the Gini coefficient had increased to 0.55 – more unequal than the USA at 0.42. However, poverty has also declined in China. Taking the World Bank's definition of extreme poverty as meaning workers earning less than $US1.90 a day at 2013 values, in 1990, 60% of the Chinese population were living in poverty-stricken households; by 2016, that level had dropped to 1.9%. Chinese life expectancy at age 0 was 69 years in 1990; in 2016, it stood at 76 – one year higher than US life expectancy had been in 1990. In 1990, 5.4% of Chinese children died before they had reached the age of 5 years; in 2016, it was 1.1% (the same as the USA in 1990). In 1990, only 37% of those of secondary school age were enrolled at school; by 2016, that figure had reached 94% (slightly higher than the USA in 1990, which had been 91%). These achievements came at a price, mainly in air pollution. In 1990, Chinese industrial, transport, heating and other activities generated 2.17 metric tonnes of carbon dioxide per inhabitant. By 2016, this had risen to 7.55. (The equivalent figures for the USA were 19.32 and 16.4.)

The studies by Bourguignon and Milanovic cited above tackle what the latter terms the paradox of inequality: inequality has declined across the world as a whole, but increased within most countries. Although global real per-capita income increased between 1988 and 2012, the world's very poorest saw no improvement. The global middle (i.e. the 45th to 65th percentiles of the world's income distribution, mainly found in China and other industrializing countries) saw a major improvement in their living standards, but the 80th to 95th percentiles (broadly, the western middle class) experienced some decline. The richest 1% in the world, on the other hand, saw a massive improvement in their standards, and now account for 29% of all income and 46% of all wealth.

One of the main industries in which China and some other developing countries have had a particular impact on world trade is that of crude steel. (Others include low-value-added clothing and textiles, and light consumer goods.) Steel has been particularly problematic following the recent slowdown in China's economic expansion. It is estimated that the country will need to shed over a million jobs in steel-making over the next few years. Meanwhile, it has been accused by the EU, the USA and others of dumping steel at heavily subsidized prices. That kind of action is prohibited by the World Trade Organization, and cases are pending, but charges are not easy to prove, and the processes take time. In the meantime, there is panic about the effect of the alleged dumping on production in the advanced economies. Setting those issues temporarily aside, it is clear that China and India have had a major impact on global steel production in recent decades. Table 1 shows changes in production between 1990 and 2016 for today's leading steel producers (China, Japan, the USA and India), as well as two European countries (Germany and the UK) and the EU as a whole.

As can be seen, by far the greater part of China's steel production is for internal use. Not shown here is the fact that, after the USA, the main net importers of steel are other developing countries: Vietnam, Thailand, Indonesia and others. It is quite erroneous for western observers to believe that, if only globalization had not taken place and trade had remained limited to the western economies and Japan, their traditional industries would have remained at the size they were in the 1980s; we would not have benefited from exports to these growing economies. There has been a decline in *employment* in steel production in the advanced countries. Recent years have been affected by the continuing consequences of the 2008 financial crisis, but even if we go back to the pre-crisis year of 2005 (when Chinese steel employment stood at 3.5 million), there had been major decline since 1990, the Organisation for Economic Cooperation and Development (OECD)[11] calculating that, between those years, employment in the sector in Japan had declined from 310,000 to 190,000; in the USA, from 205,000 to 125,000; in Germany,

Table 1 Crude steel production, million tonnes

	Crude steel production, million tonnes			Exports/imports, 2016		
	1990	2016	Change (%), 1990–2016	Exports	Imports	Trade balance
China	66.35	808.40	1118.39	108.1	13.6	94.5
Japan	110.34	104.80	–5.02	40.5	6.0	34.5
India	14.96	95.60	539.04	n.a.	n.a.	
United States	89.73	78.5	–12.52	9.2	30.9	–21.7
Germany	38.43	42.10	9.55	n.a.	n.a.	
United Kingdom	17.84	7.60	–57.40	n.a.	n.a.	
All European Union*	191.8	166.20	–13.35	29.4	40.4	–10.5

* All-EU figures include Germany and the UK, and are for 1990 and 2015.

Source: World Steel Association, 2017. *World Steel in Figures.* Brussels: World Steel Association.

from 125,000 to 75,000. However, productivity had been increasing over the same period. In 1990, the average US steel worker produced 401 tonnes of crude steel; by 2005, it was 800 tonnes. The equivalent figures for Japan were 380 and 610 tonnes; for Germany, 380 and 600. In other words, the extraordinary rise in US steel labour productivity more than accounts for the industry's job losses; in Germany and Japan, productivity gains account for most of them.

Withdrawal of China from steel production would not bring those jobs back. It is possible that automation might have been slower without globalization, as with little competition firms might not have bothered to improve productivity, but would have gone on using inefficient methods, to the cost of their customers. With reduced automation, there would have come labour shortages, which would have been good for wage earners in the sectors concerned, but at the expense of high prices, and probably reduced innovation, as old sectors using old methods would have held on to human and capital resources. This picture is recognizable – it resembles the economies of the Soviet bloc, which did not engage in foreign trade except in accordance with plans made in Moscow. We now know that such economies become very backward and present consumers with restricted choices and poor quality.

Employment and migration

Looking beyond steel to the whole economy, there has been some decline in overall employment rates since the early 1990s, but these are not confined to the advanced countries and are very small. Data from the International Labour Organization (ILO) show the employment rate for the population aged 15 to 64 declining marginally across high-income countries from 56.5% in 1991 to 56.2% in 2016.[12] The decline was concentrated on men (from 68.4% to 64.0%), the rate for women *growing* from 45.3% to 48.5%. Across the world as a whole, employment declined from 62.4% to 59.2%, and affected both genders. The decline in China was in fact considerably greater, from 75.4% to 67.3%, and again affected both men and women. Unfortunately, global data are available only for this 15–64 age range, which is becoming of decreasing use when so many people over 15 are in education. World Bank data show that, across the world, the proportion of children of secondary school age who were enrolled in school rose from 52.53% in 1991 to 76.42% in 2015. The figure for China rose from 39.63% to 94.29%; for India, from 37.29% to 73.97%. Wealthier countries were already close to 100% in 1991, but the numbers have continued to rise. Global enrolment in tertiary education has risen from 13.84% in 1991 to 35.69% in 2015; in China, from 2.93% to 43.39%; in India, from 6.09% to 26.88%. There has also been considerable expansion of higher education in the wealthy countries.

Since 2001, the EU has standardized an employment count for the age range 20–64 for its member states, which is a more realistic estimate of the size of the potential labour force.[13] Experience varies among countries, but, overall, employment in the EU rose from 66.9% in 2001 to 71.1% in 2016, despite the 2008 financial crisis and 2010 Euro crisis happening between the two dates cited.

Although employment in most developed countries has thrived, this has often been at the cost of increasingly precarious employment conditions, as Guy Standing has described.[14] Young people are often able to find only temporary jobs, or have contracts that pay them only when an employer calls them into work (what in the UK are called 'zero-hours contracts'), or which treat them as self-employed. In a study of the US labour market, Ale Kalleberg[15] showed that, between the 1970s and the early years of the present century, there had been a major increase in temporary, self-employed and low-paid jobs in the USA. He listed a number of factors behind this development. Globalization and immigration were included, but others were improvements in technology that had created a labour surplus, and deliberate political choice by successive US governments to deregulate labour standards and to fail to increase minimum wages. Crouch[16] calculated that, in 2012, in EU member states plus Norway, anything from 33% (Norway) to 71% (Greece) of workers were either without work, temporarily employed or self-employed. While some self-employed workers are content to be such, including some very well-rewarded professional practitioners, a high number of self-employed usually indicates people either unable to find standard employment or being described as self-employed by those for whom they work in order to avoid various employer obligations.

There is considerable debate over whether part-time workers should automatically be included among those in precarious or otherwise undesirable labour-market conditions, as many people work part-time by choice. There is even complaint that, in some countries, there are inadequate opportunities for part-time work, reducing women's labour-market participation in particular.

Calculations have been made, for OECD member states, of the number of part-timers saying that they are working part-time only because they cannot find full-time employment.[17] If we add these to the existing statistics, we find that in 2012 the proportion of the population aged between 20 and 64 who were not in standard employment was above 70% in Greece, Italy and Spain; above 60% in Ireland, Poland and Portugal; above 50% in Belgium, Finland, France, Hungary, the Netherlands, Romania and Slovenia. Nowhere was it below 37%.

Another widely used measure of unsatisfactory labour-market conditions, despite reasonably strong overall employment levels in most countries, is the number of young people not in education, employment or training (known as NEETs). Of course, many young people are in employment, but in temporary or otherwise precarious and unsatisfactory positions; but the NEET statistic tells us about something even more desperate: young people simply lost to a future place in the economy. According to OECD statistics,[18] in 2016 the number of NEETs reached over 20% of young people aged between 15 and 29 in most of southern Europe (Greece, Italy and Spain) and also in Mexico and Turkey; over 15% in France, Hungary, Poland, Portugal and Slovakia; and over 10% in Australia, Belgium, Canada, the Czech Republic, Estonia, Finland, France, Latvia, Lithuania, New Zealand, Russia, Slovenia, the UK and the USA.

Further signs of the burdens being placed on workers in the contemporary economy appear in the concerns being raised about work stress, as found in research by the European Foundation for the Improvement of Living and Working Conditions (EuroFound).[19] It is difficult to appraise whether there have been actual changes or just increased consciousness – though the fact that EuroFound identified more evidence of stress in poorer EU member countries than in wealthier ones with strong welfare states suggests that this is not a case of a 'rich country problem'. People in many different kinds of work are reporting various combinations of physical and mental stress in their jobs, including difficulties in managing a balance between work and the rest of life.

All these developments reflect a change in the relationship between supply of and demand for labour, though by no means all result from globalization. There would have been pressure to substitute machines for human workers as a result of technological opportunities. Nevertheless, globalization has certainly played a part in producing a world-wide labour surplus, which logically must find at least short- and medium-term expression in reduced work incomes and worse working conditions in already-industrialized countries. Globalization's role here takes two forms: changes in the occupational structure, and immigration.

First, the shift of much productive industry to newly industrializing countries means that in wealthy countries work has to be found mainly in services. For many people this means skilled work in more congenial conditions than in manufacturing. There has been a general improvement in education standards in wealthy countries, enabling many younger people to move into these more rewarding, up-market jobs. However, for low-skilled workers, the situation is different. As the German political scientist Fritz Scharpf demonstrated back in 1991, production industries improved the productivity of such workers by putting technology at their disposal and enabling them to enjoy good wages and job security.[20] While there is technological support for workers in some services sectors, and this has increased considerably with information technology, it is less significant than in manufacturing. For some other low-skilled workers, there used to be employment in public services – jobs that did not pay much but which offered considerable security. That has declined as conditions in public employment have become tougher as a result of reductions in government spending. This has been a consequence partly of neoliberal ideology, partly of declining tax revenues consequent on reductions in taxes on corporations and the global rich. These reductions are in turn partly a consequence of competition among governments to attract transnational corporations and wealthy individuals by offering them low taxes. This is an aspect of globalization. Albeit indirectly, therefore, globalization is partly responsible for the decline in good jobs. For a time at the end of the last century, it seemed that these changes would result in mass unemployment. Eventually, however, there occurred a growth in services jobs for low-skilled and moderately skilled people, who have had to compensate for their poor skills by accepting precariousness and insecurity.

Second, globalization is responsible for much of the migration that has taken place in recent years, whether this happens through freedom-of-movement provisions such as those in the EU, corporate recruitment plans, governments encouraging immigration to resolve labour shortages and improve a country's demographic profile, or the illegal immigration that inevitably takes place when there are large disparities between income levels in different countries and mass transport is reasonably available.

It is often argued that immigrants reduce wages, since it seems clear from elementary economic theory that an increase in the supply of labour without a concomitant increase in its demand will lead to a reduction in its price. Immigration is here just one of a number of potential sudden increases in labour supply. Others include the major increase in female employment that has taken place, and internal migration from depressed to flourishing cities and regions. In all such cases, it might seem rational to seek to boost wages by restricting access to the labour market (as was often done by early trade union movements). But the evidence is against these expectations. In the 1980s and 1990s, and especially after unification, Germany tried to restrict labour supply by not reducing barriers to women's entry into the labour force. In contrast, the Scandinavian countries and the UK took steps to make it easier for mothers to work. The German labour market stagnated, but those of Denmark, Sweden and the UK flourished. Eventually, Germany changed its approach.

The reason for the paradoxical result is that the simple model of an increase in labour supply tells only part of the story. An increase in the supply of working people means an increase in the number of consumers, and therefore an increase in demand. The impact of this varies considerably across sectors. Where there is already a strong supply of local labour and rather inelastic demand, the short-term impact of immigration is likely to lead to a reduction in wages, but there are other scenarios. For example, in seasonal agriculture (a major sector for immigrant labour), there are often shortages of local workers, if only because it is difficult for people living within a wealthy society to get by on seasonal wages. It is easier for an immigrant from a poor country, who can go home during the off-seasons, living in a cheaper economy on savings from the income received. These workers have no negative impact on local wages in the country to which they come, but their spending in the local economy may boost the wages of others there; they also contribute tax payments to the national economy. The fact that they are willing to work in a seasonal pattern and for wages unacceptable to people in that economy keeps the prices of fruit and vegetables low, raising the value of the wages of others. Were the immigrants to be prevented from coming, the sector would probably move to another country, the first country losing the consumer spending and tax payments of the immigrants it has rejected.

In other sectors, immigrants perform highly or moderately skilled tasks where there are shortages of local labour, either because there has been inadequate training or because the work is unattractive. This is the case with many activities in the hospitality, health and care sectors. If immigrants were not available, employers might have to raise wages in order to recruit local staff. However, consumer demand (or, in the case of public services, government willingness to fund) may be inadequate to raise wages. In that case, the result of a labour shortage is simply a reduction in supply of the service concerned. Many restaurants and care centres would close if immigrants were not available to work in them. Further, although, if the supply of suitable local labour is insufficient and cannot easily be increased, the result of employers outbidding each other to recruit from a small pool will certainly increase wages in the sector concerned, there will be an increase in prices for everyone else. Under conditions of tight labour supply, one person's wage increase is another's price increase. The pursuit of *generally* higher incomes through the enforcement of labour scarcity is a self-defeating project.

It is true that, in some cases, labour supply could be increased by improving training, and that the availability of already-skilled immigrants might enable employers to avoid investing in training. This will be effective mainly in medium-skilled sectors, where skills can be imparted quickly enough to address current shortages. For more highly skilled activities, where training lasting several years is needed, the incentives do not work. A current crisis in recruiting hospital nurses cannot be met by launching a new training programme. Incentives to provide training for such occupations has to come from outside current market pressures, which is why so much training of this kind is either provided by public policy or becomes an unresolved problem leading to permanently reduced activity in the sectors concerned. Immigrants can rarely be 'blamed' for employers' and governments' failure to train.

If it were really the case that reducing the supply of labour was a positive move, then we should find that towns and regions experiencing sudden population loss should have the most vibrant local economies. In reality, we find the opposite. Declining labour means declining consumption, therefore a decline in demand, therefore lower wages, therefore more population loss as people emigrate, in a continuing spiral. Immigration is just part of the general issue of free trade in free markets: free economic activity is a positive-sum game, but it does throw up problems, difficult moments when the speed and size of change create insecurity in people's lives. These problems must be addressed by specific policies, not by overall rejection of the free trade model. In the case of immigration, threats to wage levels (if they exist) can be met through minimum wage policies. Inadequacies in training can be met through public training policies. The free-movement rules of the EU are a good example of this approach: there is free movement, but it is subject to certain conditions that member states can apply if their labour market stability is threatened by immigration. This is an issue to which we shall return in the final chapter.

But opposition to immigrants is rarely just part of the general issue of free trade in free markets. Immigrants come from ways of life different in various ways from the local one. It is incontestable that some people feel uncomfortable in the company of people from other cultures. Therefore, against the advantages of immigrant workers has to be set the turmoil caused if political movements succeed in stirring up hostility towards them. Experience in many countries suggests that hostility subsides when immigrant families have been settled for two or more generations and, paradoxically, where their numbers are highest. Friendship and family bonds form across the ethnic and cultural divides, people of different appearance become taken-for-granted sights in the high street and at sporting and other events. Immigrants are most likely to be the victims of xenophobic campaigns when there is a sudden increase in their numbers; when they come as seasonal workers who return home at the end of seasons and never settle; or in areas where they are not found at all, but xenophobic movements are able to spread rumours about these strange creatures whom no one has actually seen. In the US presidential elections of 2016, support for the anti-immigrant candidate Donald Trump was highest in areas with the lowest levels of immigration. In the UK referendum on EU membership of the same year, where hostility to immigrants was central to the anti-EU campaign, the vote to leave was highest in areas where there were very few immigrants, where they were mainly employed in seasonal agriculture, or where their numbers had suddenly increased. Votes for the anti-immigrant party Alternative für Deutschland in the 2017 German parliamentary elections were highest in eastern, formerly state-socialist regions where very few immigrants live.

It is important to consider at what point hostility to immigrants and the settled ethnic minorities who are inevitably included in the attacks on the newcomers does damage to the fabric of a society that outweighs the economic, cultural and demographic benefits they bring. In some countries, that hostility has already changed the political context, from time to time bringing extreme nationalist and anti-globalization parties to government office in Austria, Denmark, Finland, Hungary, Italy, the Netherlands, Norway and Poland, and to play a major role in France, Sweden and elsewhere. The USA has a president closely associated with anti-immigrant and anti-Islamic organizations; and the UK embarked on a process of ending its over forty years' membership of the EU, without at the time having a clear alternative in mind, largely because of hostility to EU freedom-of-movement policies. Globalization is a major cause of migration; hostility to immigrants is currently threatening the viability of globalization. This is the vicious circle currently confronting the protagonists of globalization.

Indirectly relevant to the issue of immigration are some negative consequences attributed to globalization experienced primarily by older men, former employees of the traditional industries rendered uncompetitive by the rise of the new economies. They have seen the activities in which they took pride decline, and their traditional communities collapse. Even if new jobs have come to their areas, they have often been in non-prestigious services activities, and more often for their daughters than for their sons. The heavily male base of employment in manufacturing and mining is not reproduced in the majority of services sectors. This more gender-balanced workforce is welcomed by many people, but for those – especially, but not only, men – brought up in communities based on those sectors and the patriarchal gender relations associated with them, the experience can be disorienting. Further, with the exception of the public-service professions (e.g. health, education), which tend to be distributed evenly across populations, those services activities that provide highly skilled, highly rewarded jobs tend to be concentrated in capitals and a small number of other dynamic cities. Unlike agriculture and much manufacturing, many services activities (especially those based on information technology) have no geographical constraints to their location. Originally, geographers had thought that this would lead these sectors to be evenly distributed across population centres, but the evidence suggests that the opposite happens: because they can choose where to locate, firms tend to cluster in generally attractive places. Because their space needs are typically low, the effects of this clustering on land prices are relatively slow to develop. Only rarely do old industrial cities become the focuses of these new activities. One consequence of this is that the best-educated and most highly skilled young people move away from declining industrial areas to the new centres of employment, leaving behind an increasingly despairing population.[21]

It is here, in these specific industries, cities and regions, and in the ugly social environment confronting many immigrants and members of ethnic minorities, that we find the negative impacts of globalization in the existing advanced economies. Viewing the issue in this way reveals the damage that globalization has produced, but also the positive impact of innovation, growing wealth and cultural diversity in other locations and sectors. These are usually cosmopolitan places that have attracted immigrants from around the world, making their contribution to innovation and diversity. To seek to turn back the clock on globalization is to seek to put an end to this dynamism. But the 'forgotten' cities and regions remain a major challenge.

There is a similar problematic imbalance in the newly industrializing countries. Longevity, health and education have improved for millions of people in China and other parts of Asia, but workers in the rapidly developing manufacturing cities are suffering from harsh labour regimes and heavily polluted atmospheres. They have been uprooted from farming areas where they were poor and lived highly restricted lives, but where they often had settled communities. In their mobility to new, growing industrial areas, they have shared the dislocation and disorientation of people left behind in the old industrial areas of the western world.

The Economy

A race to the bottom?

Central to criticisms of globalization for many on the left has been the complaint that it enables multinational corporations to play countries off against each other in the so-called 'race to the bottom', threatening to cease production in those with strong labour laws or high corporate taxes. If the logic of the race to the bottom fully prevailed, there would no longer be any private-sector employment in the strong welfare states of north-west Europe; everything would have fled to the low-wage dictatorships of the Far East or to countries with the poorest labour standards. But corporations often want the good-quality human and physical infrastructure that only relatively high-tax regimes and high-quality labour can provide. Such countries continue to be very successful in attracting foreign direct investment. Against this, it is also the case that across most advanced economies the burden of taxation has shifted from capital to relatively low-paid labour over the past three decades – evidence that important aspects of a race to the bottom have been in place, increasing inequality and reducing the money available for public services and infrastructure projects.

On the other hand, globalization is far from owing all its existing achievements to neoliberalism. A World Bank study in 2001[22] found that major factors favouring the increased participation of developing countries in world trade were reductions in transport costs and improved communications through information technology. These are technological rather than political changes – though reduced transport costs have led to more goods being carried farther around the world with no regard for atmospheric and marine pollution costs. The Bank also tried to analyse why some parts of the world had managed to benefit from world trade, while others (especially Africa) had not done so. Successful countries had spent public money on infrastructural developments, including such human infrastructure as expanded education and improved health – social democratic rather than neoliberal priorities. They had also improved the reliability of the rule of law. Meanwhile, countries that had not done these things were vulnerable to negative developments that made their position worse. The two main ones can be laid at least partly at neoliberalism's door. First was a vicious spiral: if countries were doing badly, they suffered from financial flight, which made their predicament worse. The freedom of capital movements that is a fundamental feature of neoliberal 'reforms' makes this kind of destabilizing change more likely to occur. Second, failing to enter the world manufacturing economy, but often rich in the mineral resources on which that economy depends, these mainly African countries became increasingly dependent on earnings from mineral exploitation. Wealth is gained from mineral exploitation by controlling the land in which the minerals are found. For countries with low levels of law enforcement and poorly defined borders, this has led to a major increase in civil wars for control of mineral deposits, further weakening national economies. This might have happened under any economic regime, but the dominance of neoliberal policies made it difficult for governments in poor countries to protect their economies from fitting in with whatever fate participation in global markets assigned to them. Forests and other natural environments have been destroyed, ecological balance disturbed, and diseases spread across the world, as governments have searched to engage their countries in the global economy, and as elites have sought to share in the rich pickings that such engagement brings. Global neoliberal hegemony allowed them to do this without taking social and environmental costs into consideration.

However, western opponents of globalization, particularly those who profess humanitarian concerns, need to ask through what means other than globalization it would ever be possible for billions of people outside the advanced economies to emerge from poverty. While their countries faced forbidding tariffs and controls over markets, excluding them from western economies, they could develop only through endogenous growth, which in turn required their own protectionism to prevent their infant industries from being swamped by goods from the advanced economies. Their achievements were, with very few exceptions, meagre: cut off from innovations taking place elsewhere in the world, their leading firms relaxed behind tariff walls and political favours. Had such a world continued without the series of reforms starting from the GATT and culminating in the WTO, poor countries would have remained excluded from prosperity.

Increased trade has also brought strengthening relations of all kinds across much of the world; this is the other side of the coin of cultural challenge represented by immigration. People have learned more about other countries, travelled to them, adopted some of their customs, eating habits, social attitudes and cultures. These flows have been multi-directional, but in particular people in poorer countries have been encouraged to want to know more about richer ones, and some have migrated to them. Within the EU single market, this has been particularly easy, leading to major flows from central to western European countries; but it happened to the USA too.

The illusion of economic sovereignty

Globalization has reached a point where it is not even possible to distinguish clearly between an export and an import, despite the Quixotic attempts of international and national statistical bodies to do so. Within global supply chains, a finished complex product, like a motor vehicle, accumulates components from a number of countries, often being exported and re-imported several times during the process. A joint research effort of the OECD and the Council of Nordic Ministers, published by Statistics Denmark,[23] demonstrated the impossibility of separating individual national economic efforts from 'the rest of the world'. The Nordic economies are, of course, small, but the OECD has calculated the import content of exports for a wide range of countries, showing that even for large economies this can be high[24] – for example: China 29.4%, Germany 25.4%, the UK 21.9%, Japan 18.2%, the USA 15.3% and Russia 13.7% (2014 statistics). Desmond Cohen has argued that, when these data are put alongside the widespread sub-contracting of public-service delivery to international firms that has occurred in several countries, as well as the compromises that have to be accepted in international trade deals, the idea of economic sovereignty in the modern economy is no longer viable.[25]

An instructive illustration of this point concerns the different attitudes of British supporters of leaving the EU in favour of seeking a special trading relationship with the USA over the questions of chlorine-washed chicken and the regulation of banana quality labelling.[26] Chlorine-washing of chicken is among a number of chemical processes used in US agriculture that are banned under EU regulations, but which at least some members of the British government are willing to accept as part of a trade deal with the USA. For present purposes, substantive issues of US abattoir hygiene standards are not important. The question is whether changing one's food standards, not because one wants to do so, but in order to secure a trade deal with a far more powerful country, is a compromise of sovereignty. Not so, in the view of British advocates of a trade deal with the USA. The very same advocates do, however, see agreements reached among EU member states – including the UK itself – on trading standards as affronts to sovereignty. The main example that they have used to symbolize this is EU regulations designed to ensure that there is a common standard across the EU in defining a Grade I or Grade II banana. This is seen as an affront to sovereignty, because it prevented the UK from having its own banana classification. But the rule was not 'imposed' on the UK; its representatives were among those involved in making it. Why is there a difference in attitude in the UK to the two forms of acceptance of a food-quality rule, one via a trade agreement, the other by means of a jointly agreed rule? This is not a case of a preference among British nationalists for dealing with countries in what they have started to call the 'Anglosphere'; the UK is clearly willing to make post-Brexit trade agreements with the EU, and if such a deal were to involve continuing to use EU banana nomenclature, there would be no objection. The difference in the chicken and banana cases is the procedure through which the agreements are reached, and that is what takes us to the heart of British – and probably other – misguided understandings of sovereignty.

In a trade deal between countries, both sides want something from the other and are willing to compromise to get it, sometimes having to offer something about which they are not too happy; the overall deal makes that worthwhile. But they remain separate countries, they sit on opposite sides of the table, and do not share much common information. When an organization like the EU makes a regulation, there will also be different interests among countries and compromises that are not always happy, but what is being reached is not a deal between separate parties, but a jointly produced and agreed regulation, on the basis of shared technical and economic data, with everyone concerned having rights to oppose and object, but in the end accepting a group decision. It is that quality of sharing and joint production that seems to offend the idea of economic sovereignty.

Economic treaties of all kinds involve compromises of independent decision-making, and participation in the modern world economy requires large numbers of these. Moves to shared decision-making rather than just across-the-table deals are among the main means available for bridging the gap between political debates and decisions, which remain obstinately national, and economic rule-making, which is fundamentally transnational. To see these means as uniquely compromising is to refuse to use a valuable political instrument, preferring an idea of sovereignty derived from military concepts of earlier centuries. In an increasingly integrated world, countries gain from pooling their sovereignty in order to secure transnational regulation of economic forces.

The Economy

Conclusion: the balance sheet of globalization

Had globalization not taken place – had we, that is to say, remained in national fortress economies, with carefully monitored trade and tariff walls, strict limits on foreign travel and even stricter ones on immigration – most of the world would today be considerably poorer; the amount of *illegal* immigration, with all its consequences of increased criminality, would have been greater; relations among states would have been more hostile. On the other hand, there have been casualties from globalization: some world regions (mainly most of Africa) have been left out, and we have all been presented with general political, cultural and social challenges, the full extent of which we still have not experienced. Even in the rich countries, there have been losers – cities and regions that have not shared in the overall gains, and many workers who have experienced declining standards of security. The main winners have been the planet's richest people, with an overall increase in inequality, especially between the very rich and everyone else, partly through changes in taxation as countries have competed to attract footloose firms and individuals, though partly through changes only indirectly linked to globalization. There have been further major negative side-effects, including environmental damage.

Nevertheless, were globalization now to go into reverse, the world would become poorer, which would bring its own conflicts within countries, and intensify tension among them as governments and businesses would see the erection of trade barriers by others as hostile acts. It is not possible to withdraw from an open trading relationship without the action being perceived as unfriendly by those from whom a country is separating itself, leading to a further deterioration in relations. The UK government discovered this as it tried haplessly to argue to the EU that its decision to leave it was not an unfriendly act. For rich countries to surround themselves with new protectionist walls would not only hurt producers in the developing world, but also lead to major increases in prices and restrictions of choice for domestic consumers. Severe restrictions would have to be placed on the movement of goods, persons and capital to prevent citizens and businesses from circumventing such restrictions. Would it be possible to do this, especially for publics who have become accustomed to economic freedom, without imposing controls on people's lives of the kind found in eastern Europe until 1990?

There can be no simple 'return' to a pre-globalized world of autonomous national economies; even if it were clear to which decades that 'return' might refer, the world has been so changed by globalization that there can be no simple idea of 'return'. It is far more constructive to work out how in some policy fields the idea of national economic sovereignty needs to give way to one of pooled sovereignty in pursuit of a better transnational regulation of the globalized economy. In the final chapter, we shall consider approaches to confronting the negative consequences of globalization. But, for many of its opponents, the issue is not primarily economic, but something about their deeper sense of who they are as social persons, and the relationship of that identity to those of others with whom they are forced to come into reluctant contact. It is to these issues raised that we must now turn.

3

Culture and Politics

Impossible though it may be to reverse globalization and return to some vision of sovereign nations trying to minimize their mutual interdependence, that vision is currently the most dynamic force motivating much of the world. It marks, at least temporarily, a close to a period – under which most of us have lived all our lives, until now – of drives to reduce the significance of national boundaries to human exchanges, and to erect international organizations to improve cooperation. This period had in turn been a reaction against the disastrous period of intense nationalism, economic protectionism and military aggression that marked the first half of the twentieth century.

Also part of the history of nationalism, however, had been movements for national independence, not from international cooperation, but from the empires of Great Britain, France, Austria-Hungary, the Netherlands and, later, Portugal that had comprised the first wave of globalization. The European empires themselves had a complex relationship to nationhood, being the basis of intense national pride in the core nation of the empire, but also becoming multicultural and extending a kind of shared identity to subject peoples. The rulers of the British Empire liked to imitate the ancient Roman Empire and encourage the inhabitants of their far-flung territories to say *civis britannicus sum* (I am a British citizen – echoing the Roman *civis romanus sum*). By the late nineteenth century, the emperors of Austria-Hungary had begun to celebrate the linguistic, cultural and even religious pluralism of the peoples over whom they ruled. These empires were transnational states, and their rulers usually opposed the concept of '*nation* state', which implied that an identifiable nation should have its own state. But this became a highly powerful popular idea; people came to identify with what they saw as their nation, eventually struggling to ensure that such a unit would become the level at which democracy would have its most successful embodiment. In its early stages, nationalism was usually a movement of liberation, with a 'people' being pitted against a foreign aristocratic and *haut bourgeois* elite. Later, modern welfare states would be erected at the level of the nation state and given the misleading label of 'universal', because they extended to an entire people – but one bounded by a nation state.

The constructed nature of the nation state

Nationalism has, therefore, played an important progressive role in modern history, and states are very real institutions attracting strong loyalties from many people, enabling them to identify with collective goals and express generous solidarity. But this loyalty is today being mobilized by important political groups on the right to hinder the creation of effective institutions for collective governance in a world where economic power is wielded at higher levels. It is therefore necessary to explore ways in which solidarity might be able to transcend the nation state. This does not mean trying to replace it, but locating it within a *matryoshka* of political identities, where it is not the largest doll. The starting point is to demonstrate the *constructed* nature of the idea of a nation state. The very way that we use the term 'nation state' as automatically implying that states unambiguously represent single nations, and that the latter possess an unchallengeable identity, is itself deceptive. This does not make the idea any the less real; but it does imply its mutability. Human life can be governed – and sometimes needs to be governed – at other levels.

The Treaties of Westphalia (at Münster and Osnabrück) in 1648 are usually credited with founding the modern European state system, a concept of the sovereign state that was eventually exported to the rest of the world. It is not a claim that bears much examination – especially if 'state' is then understood to mean 'nation state'. The treaties, which formally ended the Thirty Years' War, did end the claim of the Habsburg family ruling the Vienna-based Holy Roman Empire to exercise power over most of the German-speaking world, and in that sense put paid to the idea of a sovereign authority over a large part of Europe. But the main victor was not a German nation state but the mass of autocratic territorial principalities, dukedoms, prince-bishoprics and city-states that then dominated German territory until the 1860s, each erecting its border controls and limiting trade with the others.[1] The German population did not share in their princes' and bishops' victory, having been devastated by the war itself and the rapine, disease and impoverishment that it brought. In any case, other major western European political formations outside Germany had already established their autonomy from the empire: France, England, Sweden, Denmark, Portugal, Poland. Spain had, too, but was linked to Austria through the Habsburg family. None of these entities constituted states with borders that can be truly called 'national'. The territory governed by the French kings had boundaries to the east and south that varied over time. The English crown ruled over the Irish and Welsh nations with difficulty, while Scotland was still a separate kingdom, though sharing a monarch with England since the early seventeenth century. The borders separating Denmark, Norway and Sweden from each other changed several times. Poland was at that period part of the Polish–Lithuanian Commonwealth, an entity with a highly variable geography that was to disappear altogether.

Neither did these seventeenth-century political formations constitute what we would today regard as a 'people'. They were the properties of rulers, and the identity of the populations being ruled over would change as military encounters came and went. At times of war, kings and their aides would incite something recognizable as national fervour in the troops they were expecting to die for them, but otherwise all that rulers wanted from their populations was obedience and taxes. They did not even care what languages they spoke. It was left to the churches to carry out many of the functions that we associate with modern government, and most churches were part of transnational organizations.

Etymologically, the word 'nation' refers to people who share a birthplace (natives), and it made sense when the Romans used *natio* (or its near-synonym *gens*) to describe the various peoples they encountered during their conquests, peoples who would rarely travel much outside a local area bounded by rivers, marshes and mountain ranges. They would therefore have very distinctive ways of life, religions and languages. In medieval Europe, the term 'nation' was mainly used to describe groups of university students from different regions, universities being then, as now, places where young people of unusually heterogeneous origins meet, providing otherwise rare occasions for different peoples to come together, not always in friendly circumstances. As transport networks improved and people started moving around wider territories, truly historic nations became less distinct. Paradoxically, therefore, the idea of nationhood grew across the eighteenth and nineteenth centuries precisely as its clarity declined. Living as we do in a period of simultaneous globalization and revival of nationalism, 21st-century people should not find that paradox hard to understand.

For people seeking liberation from Habsburg rule, it seemed logical to start with the idea of nation and then to demand that nations should be states. A major step was the identification of 'nation' with 'language' – especially as liberation movements were usually led by highly literate bourgeois cultural and intellectual groups. Johann Gottfried Herder, who is usually credited with founding European nationalism in the late eighteenth century, was primarily a theorist of language. Italians, Hungarians, Poles and Czechs (sometimes including Slovaks, sometimes not) could define themselves as language nations, and in those terms several of these movements were successful. The multicultural, polyglot Austro-Hungarian Empire (as it had been rebranded in the later nineteenth century) had not tried (or bothered?) to interfere with the linguistic complexity of the territories over which it ruled. In any case, its elite spoke French, rather than German. The more successful states of the west, especially France and England, were less accommodating. A standard French was eventually imposed on speakers of other languages within the territory conquered by the French state, such as Catalan, Basque, Provençal, Breton, as well as the country's mass of dialects – though even by the First World War French officers found communications with their dialect-speaking troops difficult. The English education system similarly drove out Scottish Gaelic, Welsh and Irish. At the same time, the English continued to recognize the Scots, the Welsh and the Irish as separate 'nations', mainly for sporting purposes. Strictly speaking, the modern United Kingdom is not a 'nation state' at all, but a plurinational state. From the Union of England and Scotland in 1707 until Irish independence in 1922 it comprised four nations; since 1922, it has been three and a half: England, Wales, Scotland and only the north-eastern part of Ireland. This continues to provide considerable complexity in sport – and when it comes to national identity, sport is no trivial pursuit: probably second only to war in its capacity to stir national passions and identities. For Association football, England, Scotland, Wales, Northern Ireland and the Republic of Ireland constitute rival nations. For Rugby Union football, there is still a united Ireland; for cricket, Welsh and Northern Irish people are expected to identify with England.

One finds the process of language construction at work even in those nations that did have a consciousness before they were able to form states. One of the first tasks of the rulers of united Italy was to establish the grammar and a standard vocabulary for an Italian language in a country of a mass of sometimes barely mutually comprehensible dialects. The Czech, Moravian and Slovak people sought the nation state that was eventually established in 1920 as Czechoslovakia. This was accompanied by a not very successful attempt to construct Czechoslovakian out of the similar but distinct Czech and Slovak languages. Since Slovakia split off as a separate state in 1993, there has been official determination to stress their linguistic separateness. The languages spoken by the people of what used to be known as the Low Countries were diverse: mainly various dialects of Dutch, Frisian, French and some German. By 1839, the establishment of Belgium as a separate state from the Netherlands only partly tidied these differences. The Netherlands remained Dutch-speaking, but had a mixed population of Catholics, Calvinists and (later) secularists living together through elaborately structured cooperation. Belgium was overwhelmingly Catholic, but divided into speakers of French and Flemish (a variant of Dutch) and a small German-language group. The difficulties that Belgians continue to have in accepting equal status for French and Flemish demonstrates the importance of national linguistic unity to nation building, even though it is found in perfect form in only a few cases.

Hungary, whose language is completely different from those of its neighbours and is not even part of the Indo-European language group, could be more confident of its linguistic particularity – except that the boundaries of modern Hungary do not at all correspond to the language boundary. There are minorities in Hungary speaking the languages of all its neighbouring countries, and vice versa. Finnish, which is very remotely related to Hungarian, is similarly associated with strong national symbolism. However, at the time of Finns' nationalist surge against Russian rule in the late nineteenth century, the majority of educated Finns, and therefore leaders of its nationalism, were Swedish-speakers, though they eagerly learned Finnish as part of the national struggle. To this day, Finns have never been able to win back from Russia the region that they regard as their heartland, Finnish-speaking Karelia.

The Reformation had made national *religious* unity highly important, at a time when churches rather than governments were the main guarantors of behaviour among ordinary people. The Treaty of Osnabrück formalized this in the doctrine of *cuius regio, eius religio* (translating loosely: to whom belongs the rule, belongs the religion). For predominantly Catholic countries, this was still (at least in principle) a matter of accepting a transnational authority. However, Protestants – and the Greek and Russian Orthodox faiths – established national churches, albeit within wider communities, such as the Lutherans. Significantly, only the English kings insisted on a totally separate national church, subordinate to the monarch alone. We can perhaps see a secular continuation of this today, with (at least in western Europe) the countries most at ease with integrating their nation states within a wider European entity being those with strong Catholic legacies. The Nordic Lutheran countries are rather less enthusiastic, while a majority of the English and Welsh have recently decided they cannot tolerate European integration at all.

Matters became more serious once the French Revolution had revealed the potential political importance of the masses, the standing armies of nineteenth-century warfare had made military mobilization more or less permanent, and industrialization had required the organization and education of whole populations. National identity and mass patriotism became highly useful, perhaps essential, to successful rule.

In a fascinating study of how states made nations in nineteenth-century Europe, Susan Cotts Watkins[2] demonstrated how, for the majority of ordinary working people and peasants, effective cultural boundaries had once been heavily restricted to areas within a day's easy travelling distance. She looked, in particular, at women's lives, and how ideas about how many children to have, and at what intervals, seemed to spread among family and friendship groups, with important changes at geographical boundaries that made conversational encounters difficult. From the 1840s, governments started to construct railway networks that linked together formerly distant areas, facilitating wider social bonds, but stopping at national borders, and so cementing various national limitations to such bonds. Growing literacy brought mass-circulation newspapers and magazines, which again usually addressed national audiences. Truly national cultures do not date back much before that period.

Modern mass media have changed this again, as global cultural conglomerates have broken down much national distinctiveness. This has often, though not always, been a case of the spread of a specifically

American culture through Hollywood films and global food chains. Ask British people what a sheriff is, and they are far more likely to refer to the Wild West than to medieval England. Most English and Italian children probably recognize the Disney portrayals of, respectively, Winnie-the-Pooh and Pinocchio, rather than the original drawings. Pizza and hamburgers may have started life as Italian and German dishes, but they became global only after American transformations.

States have certainly been highly successful in their nation-building project, but they remain constructs, not essential, immutable realities. Within modern Europe, only Portugal has national borders dating back to the fifteenth century, and only Spain to the seventeenth. Apart from Spain, the biggest European states all had major adjustments to their boundaries during the twentieth century: Italy in 1919, the UK in 1922, Poland in 1945, France in 1947, and Germany in 1945 and 1990. Many people in nations that are included in wider states seek to break away from the larger entity: for example, Catalonia in Spain, Scotland in the UK; but others in the same populations are content with the wider identity – provided, perhaps, that they have a degree of self-government within it. As many people increasingly travel around the world with different levels of passport and visa requirements, buy goods and services across great distances, enjoy each other's food, music, art, literature and fashions, and learn each other's languages, strict definitions of national belonging and limitation lose some of their power. This then creates divisions between people who have such experiences and those whose lives remained bounded by locality and nation.

The return of eighteenth-century conflicts

To understand what is happening, we need to turn back again to the eighteenth century and its conflicts, not between empires and nations, but between the *ancien régime* and the Enlightenment (*Aufklärung*), a confrontation that has had a complex relationship to the former conflict. Stated very crudely, the Enlightenment, as represented in particular by Immanuel Kant, stood for the growth of rationalism and universalism – universalism implying a kind of equality among people, however narrowly and variously this was originally conceived. In the long run, rationalism also implied willingness to change and innovate, to re-evaluate goals and the means to achieve them – a mentality that found its purest expression in the science of classical economics. The *ancien régime*, conservatism, stood for tradition, stability, unchallenged religious belief, a general abstention from questioning hierarchies and inequalities that were sanctified by time. Seen from a conservative point of view, Enlightenment values were cold, disruptive and unsettling, accessible only to the educated; those of the *ancien régime* were accessible through familiarity and endurance. As the twentieth-century English Conservative philosopher Michael Oakeshott expressed it, the conservative does not say, with Goethe's Faust, 'Verweile doch, du bist so schön' (Stay a while, you are so beautiful), but 'Stay, you are familiar to me.'[3] Liberals and social democrats who marvel at the willingness over the decades of millions of relatively poor people to vote for parties that seek to maintain a social order that keeps them poor need to view conservatism from Oakeshott's perspective: poor people often crave stability and famili-arity, and are likely to see change as threatening the little they do have.

This perspective also helps us explain the current puzzle that many of the leaders of the new conservative move-ments, outstandingly Donald Trump, claim to speak for the marginalized and downtrodden, while boasting of their own wealth and pursuing economic policies that favour the rich even further. Conservatism does not offer security through redistribution, but through the asser-tion of values, old certainties and power exercised by admired rulers. The adjective 'liberal' is always attached to the elites they criticize; they have no objections to elites in general. And the main offence committed against conservative values by liberal elites is that they support various ethnic, sexual and cultural minorities, disturbing an earlier, ostensibly more comfortable world.

As noted, nationalism was originally part of struggles for liberation from autocratic rule, and to the extent that autocracy based its authority on the sanctity of tradi-tion and even divine right, nationalist criticisms joined with Enlightenment rationalism. But the logic of ration-alism was universalist; the French Revolution declared *les droits de l'homme*, not '… *des français*'. This was rap-idly rationalized (or betrayed) through the Napoleonic formula that declared the French nation to be the bear-ers of this universalism, which it would bring to other nations through military conquest. A similar betrayal of universalism, and indeed rationalism, took place in the European nationalist movements of the late nineteenth and early twentieth centuries, and the African, Arab, Latin American and other nationalisms of the mid twen-tieth. Once independence had been achieved, there was usually a swift transition to the use of national symbols to define and defend a national elite, the suppression of criticism, and a fairly rapid move to the development of national myths. When nationalism continues to dominate a political system after the achievement of independence, it finds its centre of gravity on the romantic right.

The two axes of modern political conflict

Conflicts between conservative traditionalism and liberal rationalism became one of two great axes of conflict emerging out of the French Revolution that continue to shape our political universe today. The second was that between forces defending economic inequality and those seeking to erode it, which in practice meant a conflict within the Enlightenment bloc, between advocates of, respectively, the liberal market economy and egalitarian social citizenship. This axis developed during the nineteenth century with the rise of the industrial working class, producing the triangular conflict between conservatism, liberalism and socialism or social democracy that is found somewhere in the party structure of most long-term democratic countries, even if their meaning with reference to individual parties has often changed. If we take 'right' to signify the interests of established power and those who support the security it offers, and 'left' to indicate those who are discontented with and seek to challenge established power, we can see that conservatives always constitute the right, by definition. Social democrats constitute a permanent left, because they always seek reduced inequality, and their support base is always rooted in those lacking power and wealth. Liberals constitute the left when they are challenging conservatives on issues of traditional authority, but join with them on the right when they are defending the freedoms of property ownership.

With the retreat of traditional conservative values under the pressure of scientific rationalism, and particularly after the defeat of militarized nationalism in the Second World War, conflicts over the first axis gradually declined, though they remained important, especially in predominantly Catholic countries, for issues of family, gender and sexuality. Referendums and parliamentary votes over contraception, divorce and abortion reverberated across the world, touching very mixed and powerful emotions among groups of various political and religious allegiances. However, in general, as democracy became well established, and winning the votes of manual workers became central to political success, the second axis came to dominate. Political conflict concentrated mainly on issues of redistributive taxation and the size and scope of the welfare state.

By the late 1970s, there had been in many countries three decades of redistributive taxation and social policy: victories, even if in relatively minor ways, for the egalitarian pole of the second axis. When inflationary crises brought widespread dissatisfaction with overall economic conditions, economic liberals were able to present themselves as future-oriented challengers, advocating a move back to more inequality, against a conservative social democratic order that was increasingly on the defensive. At around the same time, the ranks of manual workers in industry began to decline with growing automation and globalization. The social democratic and socialist left was challenged in its claim to represent the population of the future. In the 1990s, the fall of communism brought new populations in central and eastern

Europe into the democratic capitalist world. This had two consequences relevant to our theme. First, it amplified the process of globalization, with production in, sales to and immigration from several countries with lower standards of living than prevailed in most western European lands. Second, it introduced to democracy new populations, many of which had a strong aversion to anything remotely resembling state socialism. This reinforced the power of conservative and liberal parties at the expense of social democratic ones both within the countries concerned and within the EU. Given this dominance of neoliberalism, European social democratic and labour parties (and the Democratic Party in the USA) began during the 1990s to accept many of its tenets. In particular, they began to neglect the concerns for redistribution and security of their traditional working-class constituencies.

While these shifts in favour of the inegalitarian pole were taking place along the second axis, globalization was bringing a return to prominence of the first, with traditional conservatism reappearing in its guise of representing stable national traditions against the disturbing changes of a liberal internationalism that was threatening traditional ways of working and living, undermining national independence and bringing large numbers of strangers into communities. The alliance between conservatives and liberals that had been fairly easy to achieve when second-axis issues of redistribution dominated was becoming fraught. On the other side, although social democracy is a child of the Enlightenment, in practice the universalism of its welfare states had been implicitly limited to the oxymoron of a national universe; and its core social supports had been industrial working-class communities. Increasingly those communities, or what was left of them, having been neglected by social democrats, began seeking refuge from globalization in a conservative nationalism, while social democracy's newer recruits among middle-class professionals allied firmly with cosmopolitan liberalism. We had arrived at a complex intersection of the two axes, playing havoc with familiar party alignments.

The Swiss sociologist Daniel Oesch was the first to notice these axial changes, in a series of publications in the early years of this century.[4] His main concern was dissatisfaction with the idea of an undifferentiated middle class, given that the category was coming to mean the broad majority of occupational positions in the advanced economies. He proposed that social and political attitudes were formed not just by the positions people occupied in organizational hierarchies (class, relevant to values on the second axis), but by the kinds of work tasks or orientations on which they were engaged (affecting the conservative–liberal axis). He distinguished three kinds of tasks: *technical* – in a hierarchy of technical experts, technicians, skilled craft workers, routine industrial and agricultural workers; *organizational* – in a hierarchy of higher-grade managers, associate managers, skilled office workers, routine office workers; and *interpersonal* – in a hierarchy of sociocultural professional workers, sociocultural semi-professional workers, skilled service workers, and routine service workers. Oesch's research concentrated on Germany, Spain, Sweden, Switzerland and the UK, but his ideas were later applied to all western member states of the EU on issues of direct relevance to us here by two German political scientists working in the USA,

Herbert Kitschelt and Philipp Rehm.[5] Together, these studies suggest that people engaged in organizational tasks were most likely to have authoritarian attitudes, those in interpersonal ones were the most likely to be liberal-minded. Particularly interesting is the fact that Kitschelt and Rehm started with three axes: attitudes to redistribution, authoritarian or liberal values regarding social behaviour, and more or less inclusive attitudes on citizenship and immigration. However, the latter two tended to collapse into one position, corresponding to our first axis: people who believed that immigration should be restricted were also likely to believe that school discipline should be tougher – a classic conservative position. This connects to an important finding of other research, carried out in the UK and the USA after the Brexit referendum and the Trump presidential election, respectively. Eric Kaufmann found that voters for Brexit and for Trump were significantly more likely than their more internationalist opponents to consider it more important that a child be 'well-mannered' than 'considerate'.[6] The difference is very subtle. The two ideas are not opposed, and it is possible to believe that both are important. However, a stress on being well mannered concentrates on control over the individual concerned; being considerate is about relations with others. This speaks to a general difference between conservative and liberal outlooks.

Reason and emotion in democracy

Seeing current conflicts around globalization as a revival of the epic struggle between the Enlightenment

65

and the *ancien régime* also enables us to understand
the rejection of the concepts of evidence and expertise
important in the Trump and Brexit campaigns. This is
the old hostility to science and reason inherent in historical conservatism, with its preference for the authority
of leaders or religious beliefs, rather than knowledge.
Michael Oakeshott, the British Conservative philosopher referred to above, was explicitly hostile to the
role of rationalism in politics: the title of his book,
Rationalism in Politics, was intended to be scornful.
It has been easy to forget the association of conservatism with such attitudes, so much did the Enlightenment
view come to dominate, through the triumph of science,
the market economy, with universal citizenship and its
associated rights. For so long now has the mainstream
political right appeared as a rationalizing, economically
neoliberal force that we forget the important role of
romance and emotion in its longer history. It has, significantly, taken an Indian author, Pankaj Mishra, to
remind the British of their and other Europeans' legacy,
in nineteenth-century *belles lettres*, of the fear of losing
honour, dignity and status, the distrust of change, the
appeal of stability and familiarity, that constitute the
tense and antagonistic emotional background of conservative ideas.[7] These values have survived, usually in
the background, carried either by religious faiths or
just by the settled customs of established communities.
Now, in the early twenty-first century, they are making
a major counter-attack.

However, there is not an epic struggle between rationalism and emotion in which liberals stand unequivocally
for reason against human feeling; nor is the suppression
of emotion a universal good. The third, often overlooked,

item in the French Revolution's secular trinity – *fraternité* – reminds us of this. Forget its gendered expression; 'fraternity' tries to convey the idea of a shared family membership of, ultimately, all human beings. By using the imagery of family relationships, it refers not just to a scientific, biological unity, or the neutrality of bureaucratic arrangements, but to feelings of human warmth and emotional attachment. Idealist though this is, it has important practical political implications. Political scientists' models of electoral participation as a matter of voters judiciously calculating where their material interests lie are far from reality. No one has the capacity to make such a calculation and sum it into a decision to vote for one candidate. Indeed, and as political science often recognizes, given the infinitesimal chance that one's individual vote in a mass election will have any effect, it is almost never rational for an individual to vote at all. In nearly all democratic systems, voting is not even a public expression of an identity, as voting is secret. It is a private act, demonstrating an association with something beyond oneself, which has to be satisfying to the voter at a level of deep feelings.

It would therefore be folly to ignore the vital role of the expression of emotion in the democratic process. Only deep emotion can stir people to take political risks and embark on bold enterprises, tasks to which the left needs to rally people at least as much as does the right. Furthermore, strongly felt community identities have supported and stabilized political identities of left and right alike: not just remnants of old aristocratic or Catholic peasant communities, but also those of coal miners, steel and textile workers. What is often fondly imagined to have been a class-wide identity that sustained working-class support for social democracy was often in practice an accumulation of far more occupationally and locally based identifications of solidarity. It was then the rationalistic task of trade unions, parties and movements to aggregate these into class-wide movements through bureaucratic structures. Emotion and reason, community identity and rational organization worked together.

Although Mishra's work on the role of anger and emotion is mainly concerned with the European conservative tradition, he also reminds us of the importance of what he calls 'spirituality', the need to connect with something deeper than economic calculation. Similarly, the Spanish socialist writer Manuel Castells has recently called for a rediscovery of the importance of values in left-wing politics,[8] a position also adopted by the late Polish socialist Zygmunt Bauman,[9] who captured in his idea of 'liquidity' that unsettling, insecure character of neoliberal society that has led so many to seek a return to old apparent certainties. Ironically, it was, in part, reformist social democrats and neoliberals, the very people who stood for – and are now criticized for having stood for – a rational, technocratic politics, who also stressed the importance of certain kinds of deeply felt identities. Anxious to retain an egalitarian rhetoric, but seeking to avert attention away from classic, 'second-axis' material egalitarianism, they defined the pursuit of equality in terms of identities – of gender, ethnic background and sexual orientation. They ignored or played down the concerns of sexually 'straight' males of the majority ethnicity; these were seen as too redolent of the old working-class past from which social democracy was believed to need to liberate itself. But it is the clamour of these last for recognition of their identity that is feeding the emergence of the identitarian right. In particular, as the Swedish sociologist Bo Rothstein has argued,[10] turning away from the social democratic tradition of a universalist welfare state, and accepting the neoliberal agenda of means testing and restricted benefits, helped produce a world of limited, focused identities.

The impact of radical Islam

One cannot give a full account of this question without considering the deterioration in relations between the west and many groups in the Islamic world. While this includes resentment against what is seen as a western economic imposition, it is also cultural. With western products and the establishment of factories and other plants by western firms come cultural norms and practices, including those concerning gender relations. Added to this have been other, partly autonomous factors: internal causes of religious hatreds and civil wars, as well as the repeated military involvement of the USA, the UK and occasionally France in those conflicts. This set of problems has produced disastrous instability in the lives of people in many parts of the Islamic world, alienating many of them from the existing world order. It has then, in turn, intensified the sense of growing helplessness spreading across Islamic minorities in Europe and the USA. Globalization is clearly relevant to these tensions, but it is misleading to blame that phenomenon for everything involved. Possibly increased sensitization to cultural identity produced by the invasion of western products and mores has intensified the mutual resentments of Sunni and Shiite Muslims, but it can hardly be blamed for the existence of those tensions, or the decision of some adherents to address them through slaughter.

While most of the suffering is being borne by Islamic people themselves, these developments have had two consequences for Europeans and Americans: a major increase in the numbers of people seeking asylum and refuge from violence and war (mainly an issue for Europeans); and the growth of isolated acts of terrorism against western cities and transport systems by very small numbers of young Muslims. Separate though they may be, these factors come together to confront some western people with the image of masses from an alien culture coming into their societies – among whom there might be terrorists. If, as was achieved by the official campaign for the UK to leave the EU, refugees, asylum seekers and terrorists can be presented as part of the same phenomenon as immigrants from central Europe within the single market, the link between globalization, Europe and the crisis over Islam can be, and indeed was – however dishonestly – presented as the same thing. In the USA, President Donald Trump makes use of anxieties about both Mexican and Islamic immigrants in a general clamour to seal the country's borders against both persons and goods.

All the xenophobic movements that are today spreading across Europe and the USA make heavy emotional use of the Islamic issue, and it is doubtful whether without this connection the negative aspects of economic globalization would alone have been enough to make the resurgence of nationalism so strong. Indeed, these movements are strongest in the wealthy countries that have gained most from globalization – the USA, Austria, the Nordic states, the UK, France, the Netherlands, Switzerland. In Germany, Alternative für Deutschland started life with a rather technical campaign against the Euro, attracting little public support. It acquired traction only when it made Islamophobia the main item on its agenda. Governments in Hungary, Poland and the Czech Republic, countries that have benefited enormously from their membership of the EU, turned up their anti-European nationalist rhetoric when they were asked to help Greece and Italy bear the burden of the refugee crisis.

The transformation of political identities

Participation in democracy requires a balance between reason and emotion. When there is too little emotion, politics becomes a dry, technocratic exercise, accessible only to those sufficiently well informed and sufficiently interested in dull detail. When emotions – and especially those of fear, rage and hate – rule without challenge from reason, politics becomes dangerous, even physically. Debate as a meaningful exchange of opinions, during the course of which people might amend their views, or at least understand those of their opponents, becomes impossible. Feelings unaided by reason are not up for discussion; one accepts them or rejects them. That cannot help democracy. If it is technocrats who dominate the world governed by reason alone, the world of emotions is ruled over by those who know how to manipulate powerful feelings. Today this is most easily done, negatively around xenophobia and positively around nationalism. It is not fortuitous that both the xenophobic western extreme right and extreme Islamists have occasional recourse to violence, and celebrate the essentially masculine nature of violence.

How can we acquire the balance between reason and emotion that we need, given, first, that we cannot spell out exactly what such a balance should look like, and, second, that such matters emerge from a mass of historical accidents beyond anyone's control? We can at least try to understand what kind of balance we have, in many western democracies, inherited from the relatively recent past, and why we might now be losing it.

For most of their lives, most people do not feel engaged in politics. It is boring, complex and remote. The rationalist model of the calculating voter is absurd and unrealistic. What has happened for much of the history of modern democracy is that we have worked out whom we regard as being 'people like us' – that is, we work out a social identity; we then find a party, or parties, that seems to speak for 'people like us'; or just notice what our parents or people living around us seem to have done; and we vote accordingly, unless the preferred party behaves badly in some relevant way. Finding the party for 'people like us' is a complex mix of reason and emotion. There is clearly a rational process of linking a party to an identity, and in noting to which identity we seem to belong, but having an identity with a group is also a matter of emotion, *fraternité*. Political identity, therefore, becomes possible when a social identity that we *feel* acquires clear political relevance. This is particularly likely to happen when that social identity becomes the explicit focus of struggles over inclusion in and exclusion from political rights – that is, citizenship: 'You are part of X and as such have rights; it is therefore important that you prevent the spread of these rights to Y, who are different and stand outside'; or 'You are part of Y, and because you are Y, those in X are excluding you from rights they enjoy; it is important that you support the struggle to share those rights.'

In the historical forging of democratic citizenship in Europe and elsewhere, two such social identities played this powerful role of enabling millions to come to know who they were politically and therefore to know how to participate in elections and related activities: social class and religion. Until the twentieth century, citizenship rights were usually limited to men, and to members of certain religious faiths, ethnic categories and economic class positions (usually defined in terms of property ownership). Groups thereby defined as excluded could be mobilized to support parties and movements campaigning for their inclusion. Groups defined as included could be mobilized to prevent extension to the excluded. Struggles over these issues were intense – at times violent. Gradually these conflicts were resolved through recognition of universal adult citizenship for persons holding the nationality of the country in which they lived. Party identities backed by strong emotions passed from being the sources of extreme division and civil strife to being the pillars of democracy. Problems have remained for some ethnic minorities, and the majority population of women often continues to lack full substantive citizenship, but in general conflicts over class and religion have been contained within the rules of electoral contest and conducted through rational discourse, while the strong party identities that had been forged in the earlier struggles continued to make electoral participation emotionally meaningful, securing the liveliness of democratic institutions alongside their stability.

As time passed, the struggles behind these solid identities became memories of parental and grandparental generations. Further, with the coming of the post-industrial economy, the occupations that had been at the heart of class identities started to disappear. Similarly, throughout Europe, religious faith has declined, again creating populations for whom the former politics of religion has no meaning. The situation is different in the USA. There, class identity was long obscured by struggles over inclusion and exclusion resulting from the Civil War of the 1860s and its associated racial politics. These conflicts took place within as well as between the two great parties of Democrats and Republicans, with the result that, for much of the twentieth century, US political conflicts seemed to be less ideological than those in western Europe. Religion seemed to have been exclude from political struggle by the Constitution's insistence on full religious liberty. In recent decades, however, continuing strong racial antagonisms have found expression in mass attachments to a variety of faiths, which have then played a political role. Contrasts between western Europe and the USA have moved round 180 degrees, with ideological and religious conflict being far stronger in the latter. The European extreme right now looks to the 'alt.right' movement in the USA for inspiration, in a similar way to how many Europeans in the 1930s looked to US liberalism for succour, and sometimes refuge.

Overall, democracy has been losing the emotional attachments that had once supported it, while politics has been becoming increasingly technocratic, especially as neoliberalism asserted the sovereignty of rational calculation of economic self-interest. This created the base for what I have described elsewhere as post-democracy.[11] But here we reach a fundamental point: among the few social identities remaining that can both have political meaning and carry powerful emotions is nationhood. It is easy for people to work out to which nation and/or ethnic group they belong; nations being political entities, this social identity has immediate political implications; these can very rapidly be translated into issues of inclusion and exclusion, belonging together or apart; globalization and immigration intensify these. There is a strong temptation for political leaders, frustrated by the gap opening between them and their constituents as a result of politics becoming technocratic, to seize on the opportunities that such a situation presents. Not surprisingly, nationality and hostility to foreigners have moved to the political foreground.

It was, appropriately, the British imperialist poet Rudyard Kipling who, in his 1908 poem *The Stranger*, expressed the fear of strangers and reluctance at welcoming them felt by many. He picked up a formulation used in Mosaic law to commend the extension of inclusion to what we would today call an immigrant – 'the stranger within thy gate':

> The Stranger within my gate,
> He may be true or kind,
> But he does not talk my talk —
> I cannot feel his mind.
> I see the face and the eyes and the mouth,
> But not the soul behind.
>
> ...
>
> The Stranger within my gates,
> He may be evil or good,

But I cannot tell what powers control —
What reasons sway his mood;
Nor when the Gods of his far-off land
Shall repossess his blood.

...

This was my father's belief
And this is also mine:
Let the corn be all one sheaf —
And the grapes be all one vine,
Ere our children's teeth are set on edge
By bitter bread and wine.

The logic of Kipling's sentiment is that peoples should be kept apart from each other, should not try to enter one another's communities – though this did not prevent him believing that the British had a right to invade and take over any part of the world they chose and include it within their empire. But existing peoples or nations are not products of nature, existing as absolutes; we are all the result of the very mixing and intermingling that Kipling viewed with such distaste. The combination of inevitable immigration and acceptance of Kipling's attitude leads to explosive situations where 'strangers' are regarded with an irredeemable suspicion. Kipling had the excuse of not knowing the nightmare of the Holocaust to which his mentality, combined with the ruthlessness of politicians advancing their careers by stirring up its latent antagonism, leads. Those living today who influence opinion have no such excuse.

More generally, the revival of nationalism and traditional conservatism has returned the first axis to prominence. Even issues like the rise in inequality, which might have been expected to belong to the second axis, have been interpreted in terms of the first: hence the paradox of billionaire Donald Trump as the hero of the downtrodden.

If a strong sense of national identity is proving to be a major focus for emotionally charged political mobilization, does anything equivalent stand on the opposing side, other than soulless rationalist cosmopolitans – motivated, if they are rich enough to exploit them, by a desire to keep global markets open; otherwise, not capable of much at all? In his book *The Road to Somewhere*,[12] David Goodhart, who has been elaborating a nationalist standpoint for the social democratic left in the UK, seems to take this position while adopting an attitude to immigrants and ethnic minorities similar to that of Kipling. He distinguishes between people of 'somewhere' and people of 'anywhere', though he uses these as extreme types and does not claim that everyone falls neatly into one box or the other. The former are mainly to be found in working-class communities, though also in traditional rural and provincial areas. They are firmly rooted in local communities, possess conservative rather than liberal values, and resent their culture being diluted by that of immigrants and other ethnic minorities. People of 'anywhere' are 'metropolitan' rather than small-town, operate in a global setting and resent the constraints of locality and their culture of origin. They are rootless, lacking in social identity, usually mobile, professional, metropolitan middle-class groups and care little for those around them. His argument very closely resembles that of the Conservative Prime Minister Theresa May, speaking to her party's conference in October 2016. Advocating the UK's withdrawal from the EU, but also seeking to reorient her party towards more support for a strong, post-neo-liberal social policy, May described people who saw themselves as 'citizens of the world' as really 'citizens of nowhere', in that they lacked the capacity for sympathy with the lives and troubles of ordinary people – a sympathy that, she implied, could be felt only for people of one's own nation. As several commentators pointed out, her argument resembled Joseph Stalin's attacks on 'rootless cosmopolitans', part of the Soviet Union's anti-Jewish turn in the late 1940s. Stalin was in turn echoing an idea used by the nineteenth-century writer Fyodor Dostoevsky, a Russian nationalist, in attacking fellow author Ivan Turgenev and his circle, who sought a European identity for Russians. Dostoevsky insisted that Turgenev must be a person who could feel only contempt for the people of his own country.

The perspective of May and Dostoevsky implies that solidarity and feelings of fellow citizenship must stop at national borders. This in turn implies that national traditions are untranslatable. We see similar thinking in the rejection by many British politicians of the idea of human rights, and the drive to bring the UK out of much of the jurisdiction of the European Court of Human Rights (ECHR) at Strasbourg (of which the UK was a leading founder member), and to institute instead a British Bill of Rights. This suggests that rights have to be nationally specific and can be interpreted only within national cultures that are more or less sealed off from each other. Even worse, moves to remove a country from transnational institutions reveal a determination to ensure that things remain that way and that wider understandings are nipped in the bud. If rights are the products of reason, it is always possible to find similarities among those of different nations. It is only if they are parts of a national psyche beyond the reach of rational discussion that they are untranslatable.

An alternative view of the identity of cosmopolitan people emerges from the research of Oesch, Kitschelt, Rehm and others cited above. The cosmopolitans they identified both were socially rooted and held values that cannot be dismissed as mere selfishness. They were located in certain kinds of occupation. The more that people had discretion in their jobs and worked directly, face to face, with other human persons, the more liberal and inclusive they were; the more their own work followed rules and routines in impersonal contexts, the less cosmopolitan they were, and the more they supported authoritarianism. What we are seeing is not a clash between 'anywhere' people and 'somewhere' people, but one between different kinds of 'somewhere'. The implicit conservative element in the quiet defensiveness of working-class communities is now being agitated by xenophobic movements, linking the defence of the welfare state to national identity and the exclusion of immigrants, and offering various kinds of social conservatism around gender, crime and discipline to restore threatened community values. Meanwhile, the new constituencies of social democracy, green politics and certain kinds of liberalism, among public-service workers and others in the educated sectors of the post-industrial economy – in particular, women – and in new coalitions with environmentalist forces, reject departures from Enlightenment values.

Conclusion: can human solidarity cross national boundaries?

The debate over nationalist or rationalist approaches to rights has interesting connections to the German concept of *Verfassungspatriotismus* (constitutional patriotism). This concept gave an important answer to the urgent question facing Germans after the Second World War: how can one love one's native land, when the idea of such a love being rooted in attachment to 'blood and soil' had become so dangerous? Can one so treasure the humanistic values of institutions and customs that one's country adopts that one can love it on rational grounds? One can perhaps see the British affection for the idea of 'British rights' in similar terms. But a rational constitutional patriotism will not insist on the untranslatability of the national quality of a constitution, as that goes back to blood and soil. It is able to see connections among the constitutional values of different peoples, and build broader, transnational solidarities. Many international institutions of the post-war period were based on that possibility – not least the ECHR.

Today, these institutions face strong challenges. The main reason for opposing transnational rights and, in particular, the capacity of transnational courts to judge them is probably less a philosophical objection to the idea of rights that transcend cultural boundaries than a practical one to a country's citizens being able to appeal to a jurisdiction over the head of their national government. In other words, it is a sub-set of the sovereignty argument: that citizens' rights should stop at national borders. At this point, it is important to recall the climate of opinion among liberal political, religious and legal elites in the wake of the Second World War. In the light of what was then known about the Nazi and Soviet states, there was a strong desire both to entrench a concept of a fundamental equality of human status, irrespective of culture and race, and to enable citizens to have a court of appeal beyond their state. There was an attempt to find institutional embodiment of the aspiration towards general human rights expressed in the French Revolution's *Déclaration des droits de l'homme*, the US Constitution, and the United Nations Declaration of Human Rights. But it was only in western Europe that anything substantive followed, with the establishment of the ECHR, and an associated European Convention of Human Rights, within the framework of the Council of Europe. The Council and Court are separate bodies from the European Union and its European Court of Justice, though today members and candidate members of the EU are required to subscribe to the Convention and accept the jurisdiction of the ECHR. As a recent study has demonstrated, the initial inspiration for the establishment of the ECHR came from conservative and Christian Democratic politicians, fearing the extension of totalitarian communism across Europe.[13] In practice, the social democrats who dominated European leftist politics in western Europe (with, for some decades, the important exceptions of France and Italy) became stalwart supporters of human rights and internationalism. For a period, there was therefore a broad consensus in western Europe about the acceptability of transnational institutions to which citizens could appeal.

This is now changing, as part of the general resurgence of nationalism. It is likely that the post-war mood of trying to transcend national boundaries remained an elite project, little understood by the majority of people. For a lengthy period, this did not matter across western Europe, the USA and other wealthy nations, as angry national sentiments seemed to have no place in increasingly prosperous and peaceful societies. The decline in the certainty of growing prosperity, the uncertainty of globalization, mass immigration and the confrontation with radical Islam have exposed the raw nerves of suspicion of both strangers at the gate and the countries of strangers. Clearly, 'nation' provides a politically powerful, historically rooted source of an identity of 'somewhere' for many people. Are the values of those who seek to transcend these limits doomed to defeat, defending an outmoded commitment to nowhere in particular?

In addition to confronting the economic issues raised by globalization, we are entering a new *Weltanschauungsstreit*: a conflict of world views. For many people there has simply been too much change: globalization, immigration, changed gender relationships, a new sexual tolerance, disobedient children, big cities, new economic sectors. These views are by no means confined to the ranks of the deprived living in declining areas. The majority of supporters of xenophobic movements in most countries are fairly prosperous, no longer young, inhabitants of smaller towns. These disparate groups are united by not feeling at ease with a rapidly changing and disordered world. Political causes making strong use of national identity have offered them something responding to deeply felt emotions of belonging and stability. Against these groups stand a generally younger, more self-confident population, more likely to see open horizons and multiculturalism as opportunities than as threats. They can feel strong emotions, worried at the consequences of xenophobia and hostility to immigrants, and celebrate the collapse of barriers between cultures. Their problem is that, in a struggle of emotions, those of fear, rage and hate, once aroused, can be so much stronger than those of welcoming open-heartedness. These latter stand a chance only in an environment where both emotion and reason are at work. And do transnational commitments have enough emotional energy to transcend the nation's demand of a monopoly of loyalty, when the latter is backed by so much political power?

4

The Future

It would be disastrous if the new nationalism spreading across the world were to succeed in reversing globalization. First, the process by which this would be done would cause a dangerous worsening in relations among nations, as the severance of long-established economic ties and the raising of new barriers implies hostility – including hostility to settled as well as recent communities of immigrants and ethnic minorities. Second, the advance towards greater prosperity among the people of developing economies would be checked, pushing them back into poverty and consequent instability. Third, since automation and robotization exist independently of globalization, people in the advanced economies would not find that the old jobs in manufacturing and mining came streaming back; instead, their economies would lose growing new markets in the developing world and therefore incur further job losses. Finally, the resurgence of nationalism is preventing us from making progress on the most important challenge to governance raised by globalization: the need for democracy to reach beyond the nation state. It is impossible, as well as undesirable, to return to a world of isolated, sovereign national economies – of countries whose citizens have little contact with people beyond their borders. If democracy remains trapped at the national level, while the great corporations regulate the global economy and communications among people, the working populations of both the advanced and the developing worlds will continue to experience the negative consequences of globalization.

Nevertheless, the negative consequences of the neoliberal form of globalization have meant that opposition to globalization in general has become a major political movement across many parts of the world, on both the political left and right.

Leftist opposition to internationalism

Given that the left has historically claimed to be internationalist, one might expect left-wing observers to oppose the neoliberal form of globalization in favour of its transnational regulation. This is the position I am adopting in this book, and has been the case for many others. The 'no global' protest movement that emerged in the 1990s aimed mainly at global neoliberalism, rather than at global trade as such.[1] It was also in no way nationalistic or xenophobic. It engaged in prominent demonstrations at symbolic meetings of the protagonists of globalization, such as the World Economic Forum in Davos, Switzerland, and various meetings of the Group of Seven (G7) richest countries. This movement peaked around 1999, but re-emerged after the financial crisis of 2008 and, in particular, following the harsh treatment of Greece by EU institutions, the IMF and banks. Since then, however, a more nationalistic left has appeared, using two serious sets of arguments. We have encountered these at various points above; it is now time to confront them more directly.

The interventionist sovereign state

The first runs as follows: confronting capitalism requires strong state intervention in the economy; the only level at which enough sovereign power can be concentrated in order to do this is the nation state; therefore, that state must be liberated from all hindrance to play this role. This reasoning is found, in particular, in arguments against the existence of the EU. Major exponents of this view are Bill Mitchell and Thomas Fazi,[2] who argue for a dismantling of the EU and urge other member states to follow the UK's example and leave the organization. They argue that the EU imposes an 'anti-Keynesian straitjacket' on economic policy, and that this 'war on [national] sovereignty has been in essence a war on democracy'.

There are several problems with this argument. First, although it is true that current EU policy for Eurozone countries imposes heavy constraints on a government's capacity to take on large public debt, and that these policies have had unnecessary negative effects on those countries' ability to resolve their problems, this is not a simple matter of the suppression of Keynesianism. Keynes's own arguments were not addressed to governments with vast chronic debts, but to those with surpluses, and nothing in the strategy of the European Central Bank (ECB) prevents the use of moderate demand management by governments that have their debt situation under control. Debts of the kind entered into by the southern European and some other countries during the years running up to the 2010 Eurocrisis were considerably beyond the bounds of responsible financial management. They became possible through the combination of the banking behaviour enabled by neoliberal financial deregulation and the inadequate rules of the Eurozone. In Mitchell and Fazi's preferred world, there would be no Eurozone, as national currencies would be restored. They do not carry out the thought experiment of what would have happened to the southern European economies had they continued to build up the large debts (of which the authors do not seem to disapprove) while holding national currencies. These currencies would have been subject to extreme speculative attack, increasing inflation and producing very large reductions in real incomes.

Mitchell and Fazi also want to see far more general government intervention in the economy, and state subsidies of various kinds. These are policies similar to those advocated by France Insoumise and the current British Labour Party. But many subsidies of the kind that left-wing critics would want to introduce would breach WTO rules as well as EU ones. The main difference is that the EU has to approve member states' interventions in advance, while within the WTO one can await post hoc legal action and retaliation. It is therefore likely that a government following the Mitchell and Fazi agenda would eventually have to withdraw from WTO agreements, too, and become economically isolated. It would find importing very costly and exporting very difficult. The result would be an economic autarchy in which a country's trade was mainly limited to itself, with the attendant risks of low levels of competitiveness and innovation. Mitchell and Fazi deny that they wish in the long term to see countries disappear behind national economic walls, and insist that, after the collapse of the EU, a new system of collaboration among independent sovereign nations could begin again. This is thoroughly disingenuous. The current push for a destruction of European and global trading regimes is everywhere led by the xenophobic right, and socialist movements wishing to join the new nationalist struggles would find themselves very much the junior partners. There is a curious unreality in the assessment by Mitchell and Fazi of realistic political prospects. They regard the EU as a priori doomed to a strict neoliberalism, while they regard it as quite possible that socialist governments could be voted into office in enough individual countries to start constructing, all over again, in a world of reanimated nationalism, an alternative Europe. Even then, it is difficult to see that friendly trading relations would return quickly to groups of countries that had just been engaged in acrimonious attempts to separate from each other, with their attendant loss of mutual trust. Mitchell and Fazi, and anyone else advocating a similar destruction of international institutions, have to accept that, at least for the medium term, they would be ushering in a world of restricted international trade and intensified mutual antagonism among nations.

The national welfare state

A second and more powerful case for a nationalism of the left comes from those observers who point out that the welfare state has always been a national project, a recognition of mutual obligations among people who consider that they share sufficient characteristics to constitute a national community, the idea captured in the Swedish concept of the welfare state as a *folkshem*. This is similar to the argument of Mitchell and Fazi, in that it regards a highly neoliberal EU as the enemy of these national creations. It goes further in pointing to the role not just of the state, but of a people and its sense of community. David Goodhart has argued that immigration weakens the welfare state by bringing into a country people from strange cultures with whom local people do not feel a shared identity and commitment to mutual support.[3] This argument embodies serious sociological insight. Welfare states are at their strongest when they express felt solidarities between people and are not just bureaucratic entitlements. Solidarity is an emotional attachment, a strong instance of *fraternité*, which usually has boundaries. Societies have often had little difficulty in extending solidarity to small numbers of immigrants. In the words of the Law of Moses: 'But the stranger that dwelleth with you shall be unto you as one born among you, and thou shalt love him as thyself; for ye were strangers in the land of Egypt.'[4] This was the sentiment rejected in Kipling's poem *The Stranger*. His blunt account certainly demonstrates why the generosity of spirit implicit in Leviticus may become harder to achieve as numbers of immigrants grow. But does this mean that it is impossible for people to learn to extend their senses of human solidarity more widely? Is it really true that the nation state presents immutably fixed boundaries, which human sentiment is unable to cross to embrace others?

A different argument for seeing the nation state as the only unit that can champion a generous welfare state can be found in the criticisms of the extension of the role of the EU made by Fritz Scharpf,[5] Wolfgang Streeck,[6] Martin Höpner[7] and other colleagues at the Max Planck Institute for the Study of Societies at Cologne. The integrative mission of the EU, they point out, leads it towards neoliberalism. The easiest way of securing uniform practice is to use the market, as the ostensibly most 'culture-free' institution, and that means securing integration by cutting out all elements of a policy that are not strictly compatible with market rules. This process, which often operates through the decisions of the ECJ rather than overt policy-making, tends to weaken welfare states, as well as institutions such as coordinated collective bargaining that have been central to the success of Nordic, Austrian, Dutch and German collective bargaining, but which are not consistent with strict neoliberal ideology or neoclassical economic theory. As a result, in recent years the EU has almost ceased to be a force compensating the losers from the neoliberal form of globalization and has instead reinforced the damage of its impact. Rather than a bulwark defending citizens against disruption to their lives, it has helped to intensify that disruption,[8] IMF researchers having found that structural labour market reforms of the kind being pursued by the EU have had damaging effects on productivity.[9]

These are powerful arguments, but it remains true that a world in which democratic policy-making remains trapped at the national level is one in which neoliberal order beyond the reach of democracy will continue to dominate the supranational economic level. This in turn heavily limits the scope of national policy in any economy-related field. If the logic of the Cologne argument were taken to the point where almost all policy-making returned to the nation state, the scope for limiting the reach of neoliberalism would actually be weakened.

There is another problem. If it is the case, as Scharpf has argued, that EU policy-making is sympathetic only to so-called 'liberal' economic regimes, why has it been the biggest example of a neoliberal political economy in Europe – the UK – which has found the EU's departure from neoliberalism so intolerable that it is leaving it? The list of EU policies that offend leading proponents of Brexit is also a list of policies that refute the argument that the EU is a purely neoliberal institution: the joint funding of public infrastructure projects targeted towards poorer areas and paid for largely by the richer member states; the establishment of various rights for workers, parents and other groups; common standards of environmental protection. The EU's critics from the left insist that the institution cannot possibly divert from its neoliberal path. To a degree this is true; but this is partly because neoliberal politics dominates so many individual member states. This will not be a permanent condition. The weight of neoliberalism within the EU policy mix has varied in the past and can vary again, while the neoliberalism of a global trading order beyond the reach of national polities is likely to remain extreme.

Far more positive is Scharpf's plea for a reassertion of subsidiarity: for European policy to rethink which policy areas need to be developed at Union level, and which could be better left to national or more local autonomy.[10] Subsidiarity, derived originally from Catholic social doctrine, is a key concept in EU policy design. It holds that higher levels of authority should intervene only when the most local levels need their support to execute policies.

There is, of course, scope for considerable debate about when such support is needed. From the perspective I am developing here, it would be invoked when lower-level authorities (including nation states) cannot adequately regulate transnational markets. Two areas of policy-making stand out in particular as ripe for this approach: the scope for extending democracy beyond the nation state, so that when a more central authority is required it responds to interests other than those of global capital; and reinforcing local communities and economies so that they can participate confidently at the global level.

Democracy and globalization

There can be no global democracy in the proper sense, but realistic progress can be made in its direction without the negative and sinister consequences that a truly global government would bring. First, there can be extensions beyond the nation state to democratic assemblies at world-regional level. Second, national and world-regional democratic levels can reach out to embrace global ones.

Transnational European democracy

To date, the only transnational parliament that the world has developed is the Parliament of the European Union. It is customary to ridicule the Parliament and wider EU democracy for two main reasons: these institutions are weak; and European institutions behaved in a highly undemocratic way during the Eurocrisis.

It is true that the Parliament has not entrenched itself among European citizens; participation in elections for it is low and declining; and its powers are limited. However, it does possess real powers, these have increased over the years, and the Parliament draws public attention to major issues affecting Europe. Its weakness is in relation not so much to the Commission as to national governments, who deal with its potential challenge to their own democratic legitimacy by trying to limit its reach. It is as impressive to ridicule the achievements of the European Parliament as it is for a grown adult to ridicule a baby's efforts to walk. The Parliament is a relatively recent institution that tries to do something historically unprecedented: to take elections with universal adult suffrage to a public body above the nation state. Europe is also the only world region to develop democracy in a wider sense. The ECJ and the ECHR make it possible for European citizens to do something that is possible in virtually no other part of the world: to take action against their governments in supranational courts. The European Commission maintains links to business associations, trade unions, regional authorities and other civil society institutions, often superior to those that some such groups have with their national governments. For nearly forty years, British trade unions have had relations in Brussels at least as strong as those with governments in London.

Treatment of the debtor members of the Euro bloc in the wake of the financial crises of 2008–10, in particular the replacement – at the insistence of the Commission, the ECB and the IMF – of the prime ministers of Greece and Italy, was certainly a bad moment for European democracy. However, the fundamental flaw in the architecture of the single currency was not a problem of democracy but of neoliberal economics.

Economists were able to convince policy-makers desperate for a simple solution that ending the capacity to devalue would be enough to ensure that governments behaved responsibly within the single currency, and that there would be no need for more complex arrangements at the level of fiscal policy.[11] As a result, too much, rather than too little, discretion was left in the hands of national governments. This laxity became a pressing danger when global finance deregulation enabled banks to fund the growing debts of governments wanting to offer their voters higher public spending with lower taxes. While one might well reject the extremity of the austerity packages imposed on the citizens of the countries concerned, some kind of reckoning had to be made. The core democratic deficits were not those of the Eurozone but of the national politics of Greece and Italy in particular, which were unable to monitor their governments' irresponsibility. Even then, the parliaments of the countries concerned could have rejected the austerity plan, kept with their existing leaders and turned back to the drachma and the lira. They chose not to do so, because they dreaded the consequences of risking those currencies in the international markets, given the high debt levels and weaknesses of their economies.

The European Parliament, as the instrument of European democracy, was unable to play a part in the Eurocrisis, because the UK government had refused to allow it or the other formal institutions of the Union to be used. Instead, ad hoc committees had to be established. Even then, it is by no means clear that northern European voters would have used their democratic powers to support offering more generous terms to the debtor countries. This is partly because their national

leaders failed to explain to them that the main benefi-
ciaries of the support offered to Greece and the others
would be German and other northern European banks.
But that was a failure of various national democracies, not of Europe. In the event, the only significant
northern voice calling for a better approach was that of
the German trade unions.

Critics of European democracy need to be wary of the
company in which they find themselves. In his intervention into the British EU referendum, Dani Rodrik, the
economist who has made probably the most constructive
contributions to the debate over globalization, quoted
with approval the attacks on the democratic qualities of
the EU by the British Conservative journalist Ambrose
Evans-Pritchard.[12] Evans-Pritchard insisted that the
'Brexit vote is about the sovereignty of Parliament and
nothing else.' However, in the wake of the referendum,
the British Conservative government and commentators
have developed a novel theory of anti-parliamentary
democracy, with no critical response from Evans-
Pritchard. The referendum result, the government
maintained, implied an end to any debate about the
issue of UK membership of the EU. When the Supreme
Court ruled that the referendum result could not, as the
government had argued, prevent Parliament from decid-
ing whether to accept the government's final Brexit deal,
the judges concerned were attacked as 'enemies of the
people' by the *Daily Mail*, a newspaper close to the government, with some ministers echoing the words. The
government also attempted to rule that any actions it
would subsequently take to implement post-Brexit legi-
slation could be done without reference to Parliament.
Evans-Pritchard is also a prominent advocate of the

view that Brexit provides an opportunity for Britain to become the 'Atlantic Singapore'. He was mainly extolling Singapore's weak labour rights and primitive welfare state, but the island is also noted for its flawed democracy, ranking 69= in the Economist Intelligence Unit's ranking of democracy among the 167 states for which it collects data. As the German-American political scientist Yascha Mounk has argued in his recent book *The People versus Democracy*, the democratic credentials of the new populists are often very dubious.[13]

When Jacques Delors was president of the Commission in the early 1990s, he fully understood that creation of the European Single Market also required a more social Europe. His understanding was the exact reverse of that of one of his prominent colleagues in constructing the Single Market, Margaret Thatcher. For her, the expansion of the market made it possible to shrink the social state. Delors understood that markets can destroy society unless their impact is cushioned by social policy. European social policy prospered during his presidency, though Thatcher's Britain opted out of most of its provisions. Direct relations between the Commission, regional and local governments, business associations and trade unions flourished. This legacy continued under Romano Prodi, but when the Portuguese conservative José Manuel Barroso succeeded him, European policy-making increasingly moved in a neoliberal direction, bringing it to the present position where it seems remote from the anxieties of most European citizens. At that time, the EU became concerned that weaker labour rights in the USA were the main reason for the latter's then superior economic performance. After the role that US banking deregulation played in causing the crisis in financial markets; the way in which the richest 1 per cent of US residents have monopolized the fruits of growth over forty years, leading American workers to resort to unsustainable household debt in those same markets in order to maintain their standard of living; the beating that those same workers have received at the hands of global competition; and the way in which they have started to respond politically – the long-term advantages of the US approach no longer appear so clear.

The EU still leads the world in the pursuit of improved environmental standards, though that lead has stalled in recent years, again because of fears of losing out in international competition. If the EU raised its own internal standards, it could then, as the world's largest trading bloc with which virtually all other countries in the world want to have a special relationship, insist on conformity with key social and environmental standards in trade agreements that it strikes with third countries or groups of countries. No other organization stands as strong a chance of leading the world to a more civilized globalization than the EU, which is why its leaders should proudly adopt the task, and why critics on the left who find themselves associating with campaigns on the far right to weaken it in pursuit of the chimera of a regained national sovereignty should desist from that misguided project.

If democracy is to meet the challenge of confronting economic power at the global level, it is essential that the Delors legacy is recaptured: of an EU that extends both its formal democracy through more powers for the Parliament, and its engagement with the lives and concerns of European citizens. There are already signs of such a new change of direction. Although the proclamation by the Commission of a European Pillar of Social Rights, embracing twenty fields of action, in November 2017, remains weak in its ambitions, it at least restores the idea of 'social Europe' that had been so battered in the earlier years of this century. It requires action not only from the EU itself, but from governments and various interests in the economy and civil society, but that is fully in keeping with the principle of subsidiarity. The Commission is also establishing a European Labour Authority to deal, *inter alia*, with issues of migration and atypical employment.

Theresa May's 2016 speech attacking supporters of the UK's membership of the EU targeted aspiring 'global' citizens, not European ones. This was especially odd, given that she was launching the concept of 'Global Britain' to replace the idea of the UK as an EU member. Perhaps the reason was that the EU *does* constitute, albeit weakly, a form of citizenship for the citizens of its member states. Europeans have rights and obligations in relationship to each other that are not shared by the residents of third countries. They contribute to common funds, accept the movement of persons, goods and services among each other, observe jointly made regulations, help each other's countries with infrastructure projects, can live and work in each other's countries easily, and enjoy various opportunities for jointly funded cultural and scientific activities. For several years, the further development of European social policy has been missing from the agenda. If it is now to be restored, European citizenship will engage a far wider range of people.

Europeans have three options: to work to strengthen the democracy of the EU, so that it can potentially be used to gain some democratic purchase over global deregulation – a task in which it does have notable achievements; to accept that globalization would be beyond the reach of democratic institutions, and be content to keep national democracy for minor, non-economic issues and ceremonial flag-waving; or to break from the global economy behind protective national tariff walls and regulations designed to limit trade across national frontiers. No one on the political left should be diverted from the first option of opportunities to construct transnational solidarities by the chance of jumping on the xenophobic bandwagon in order to reclaim an impossible national economic sovereignty. They should beware of the directions in which that bandwagon is taking them. A leading Marxist analyst of globalism, William I. Robinson, has pointed to the way in which capitalist interests have constructed a transnational capitalist class, not in the sense of an elite that works together conspiratorially, but as a mass of interlocking investments and ownerships that transcend any national origins or bases.[14] He contrasts this with the disorganized and fragmented working classes, set against each other by those same processes that enable capitalists to bring their interests together. Those on the left who see a further retreat into nationalism as a solution to the problem need to understand that their nationalism would work only if capital were to be required to dismantle its global structures and return to national fortresses. This it will not do.

Acceptance of the urgency of these arguments also means that public policy should avoid providing xenophobic movements with material with which to work. Immigrants can be most easily absorbed, and solidarity gradually able to include them, when they are not arriving rapidly in very large numbers. The rules on free movement in the EU's Treaty of Lisbon provide a good example of how liberalism can be combined with sensitivity to social concerns on this issue. Article 45 of the Treaty, which guarantees the right of European citizens to move around their continent, also makes this right subject to modification on 'grounds of public policy, public security or public health' (Article 45 (3)). When the UK government was seeking reassurance on its rights to control immigration from other EU countries, it was confirmed by the Commission that immigration could be limited for motives of encouraging recruitment, reducing unemployment, protecting vulnerable workers and averting the risk of seriously undermining the sustainability of social security systems.[15] Immigrants who are not economically active have no right to remain in a country if they cannot support themselves, and member states can block migration for the purpose of accessing social benefits. This approach to immigration demonstrates European policy-making at its best: seeking the economic and social advantages of liberalism (in this case, free movement), but providing means to avoid damaging consequences. No other world region has this capacity; Europe needs more of it.

Democracy and global economic regulation

However, many international issues require global rather than world-regional action. The biggest single example is, of course, climate change, but there are also issues of banking regulation, fiscal evasion and tax-rate competition. It is not possible to envisage a global set of democratic institutions. We can, however, demand a world in which national politicians freely admit that there are problems that are beyond their reach, that they need to cooperate with others within international agencies, and that therefore governments' policies within those agencies become fiercely debated within national politics. For example, is it unrealistic to imagine a general election in which an opposition made a major issue out of a government's failure to work with other countries within the WTO to suppress slavery, child labour and inhuman working hours? If Donald Trump had worked in that way instead of seeking to protect American workers from competition by protectionist measures, he would have made a major contribution to good global economic governance.

Sheer protectionism is a zero- and eventually negative-sum game, but this negative logic does not apply to policies to help launch new sectors or improve the efficiency of existing ones, not through subsidies but through investment in technology and more skilled labour. These strategies lead to the arrival of better-equipped competitors on the world market, improved efficiency and better products, leading therefore to general gains. The same is true of public policy measures to support workers in sectors being fatally wounded by globalization, providing generous redundancy and unemployment pay together with retraining, help in finding new jobs, and technical advice and support for the establishment of new sectors. These do no harm to global trade, while providing security and improved competence.

Several important studies have shown that globalization has brought some of its most effective results when it has departed from neoliberal orthodoxy. In

2002, Stiglitz[16] had already pointed out how, in the countries of South and East Asia that had gained most from globalization, governments had played a major role in supporting new industries and developing strong infrastructures through public spending. When Rodrik became the first leading economist seriously to challenge globalization in 1997,[17] he attracted considerable criticism from his profession. As he made clear in his later volume *The Globalization Paradox*,[18] he had not called for a roll-back of the process, but for what he called 'smart' – that is, judiciously regulated – globalization: heresy enough during that peak period of enthusiasm for neoliberal deregulation. He showed that the most successful period of globalization – covering what in chapter 2 we called its second and third waves – a developing free trade regime had turned a blind eye to elements of protectionism to help sectors in crisis or launch new 'infant' industries. He might be under-estimating the moral hazard that results from prolonged use of such arguments. Once the initial years of European post-war reconstruction had been completed, and the subsequent industrialization of most East Asian economies, protectionism started to become a drag on innovation and an encouragement of 'crony capitalism', and even corruption. An essentially national form of 'smartness' quickly comes up against limits. There is a need for a global governance of smart globalization, with authorities like the WTO and the EU verifying the purposes of state intervention to support and subsidize, to ensure that emerging and infant industry measures do not – as they usually do – morph into giving a few politically favoured corporations the ability to make profits without competition. The problem has been that these authorities have obeyed an over-simple neoliberal dogma to ensure the creation of free markets at all costs, not using discretion in their appraisal of cases of state aid, and encouraging a low-tax, low-public-spending political economy that inhibited positive infrastructure support. There has been a choice between global deregulation and national protection. What we need instead is smart global regulation. There are no technical problems in proceeding in this way, only political ones. The political energy for change has to come mainly from democratic demand, and that could occur if domestic politics addressed global issues as ones requiring cooperation and pooled sovereignty, not national posturing.

Even without such democratic pressure, some international organizations, especially the OECD, the IMF and the World Bank – the main protagonists of globalization – are already beginning to see the errors of earlier assumptions by neoclassical economists concerning the capacity of labour markets to adjust to global challenges without unacceptable shocks to the living standards of working people. These organizations are able to perceive these issues because they have an international perspective and no political axes to grind, beyond a certain naivety about the ability of economic theory to provide all we need to know about human behaviour. But, precisely because they occupy such a position, they lack democratic legitimacy in a world where, outside the EU, there are no democratic institutions above national level.

The WTO permits countries to join its regime of increasingly tariff-free trade provided they meet certain criteria, such as the elimination of state subsidies to firms. These rules need to be extended to include various conventions of the ILO that seek to protect working conditions. There are, in particular, eight key conventions, two each on four themes: freedom of association (i.e. freedom to join trade unions); prohibitions on the use of forced labour; similar prohibitions on discrimination against ethnic and other minorities; and others on the use of child labour. Substantive and not merely formal guarantees of trade union rights would further help workers to demand safe and healthy working conditions and reasonable working hours – though such union guarantees would be as disagreeable to legislators and corporations in the USA and some European countries as to those in China. Failure to abide substantively by ILO conventions should be as severe a barrier to a country participating in the WTO's low-tariff regime as failure to comply with free trade rules.

These things have not been done until now, partly because governments and employers in developing countries enjoy the competitive advantage that disgraceful working conditions bring, and partly because western governments appreciate the benefits for their populations of the cheap goods that they make possible. The decline in trade unions and rise of neoliberal ideology had in many countries already provoked a determination among governments and corporations to persuade citizens to see themselves as consumers far more than as workers. Having them ignore the fact that their wages were stagnating because they could buy cheap imports (and take on irresponsible household debt) was part of this.

It is true that an insistence on improvement in the labour conditions of developing countries would initially slow the speed of their economic development and restrain their employment levels, and increase the prices of goods in the west. This would, however, be merely a slowing of the process of globalization, not its reversal. And a deceleration is needed to enable working conditions in developing countries to improve, and to slow the pace of the shock being experienced by workers in the advanced economies. Economists notoriously ignore what they regard as the short-term 'frictional' costs of change, and therefore usually oppose attempts to retard its pace. It is certainly important to recognize that gradualness, like everything else, has its costs; but it reduces shocks that are destabilizing the lives of many people and the politics of much of the democratic world. More than frictional damage will be done if this instability continues to generate a revival of protectionism, nationalism and xenophobia. Rules that are tied to the achievement of clear labour and environmental standards are not protectionist, as countries can enter free trade relationships as soon as they meet an internationally monitored standard, without individual countries being able to restrict their imports on protectionist grounds.

Similar issues are raised when global corporations force governments into races to the bottom in taxation. Some governments find these races attractive, as by offering very low corporate tax rates they can encourage global firms to base themselves in their territory, benefiting from increased employment. This bubble is promising to burst as internet-based firms are turning a minor fiscal irritant into a major distortion of revenue flows. They locate themselves fiscally in countries with low tax rates without any reference to where their employees, customers or activities are based; they are not even bringing much employment with them. The countries concerned simply become conduits through which firms pass their earnings from a mass of countries to the equally varied locations of their shareholders. One can tell where this is happening: the measures of a country's gross domestic product (GDP) and gross national income (GNI) should be broadly equal. Where GDP is far higher than GNI, as is the case with Ireland and Luxembourg, money is simply winging its way through on its journey to firms' owners located elsewhere in the world, barely contributing to income in the country through which it passes.[19] The situation has now reached a point where the losses to countries who did not 'win' the races to the bottom are so great, and the gains to those that did win so small, that there will be international action on rules about fiscal location. Reduced fiscal competition among countries could also lead to a reversal of the recent tendency for corporate and capital taxes, and taxes on the geographically mobile rich in general, to be far lower than those on employment incomes, a tendency that accounts for part of the rise in inequality that has affected many countries. Capital can move itself around the world far more easily than can labour; so, in the absence of international action, it becomes far easier for cynical governments to tax workers more heavily than corporations and the wealthy. A related scandal is the use of tax havens, jurisdictions in remote parts of the world – mainly small Caribbean islands that operate under the protection of the UK government – in which companies and individuals can locate themselves legally, though in no way substantively, escaping taxation, and sometimes with a shield for criminal activities.[20] Again, governments are beginning to call for international cooperation to deal with the problem. It is a short step from here to the most urgently needed development: bringing debates over attempts at international cooperation into the heart of domestic political debate. This comes hard to governments and oppositions alike. Both like to insist that goals can be achieved at the national level alone – the former to boast of achievements, the latter to complain of failure. We need a more mature politics if globalization is to be adequately governed, with parties arguing over the policies that their governments are advocating within international organizations.

The local and the global

However, it will not be enough to cope with the negative consequences of globalization through transnational and national action. In keeping with the ideal of subsidiarity, we look to local approaches wherever these can be strong enough. There has to be local economic and social policy, not of a protectionist kind, but to enable as many areas as possible to find their way to viable economic futures, with the help of national and (in the case of EU member states) European authorities. It is only if diversity is accepted and encouraged that multiple means can be found to resolve common problems. Further, much of the feeling of 'being left behind' which is feeding xenophobia in various parts of the world can be traced back to the dismal economic prospects of former industrial areas.

Market forces in the post-industrial economy favour a small number of large cities, leaving large areas, and many – if not most – smaller cities without any dynamic activities that can sustain wealth and income, retain the young, and give people a sense of local pride in their *Heimat*. The geographical inequalities, even within countries, that globalization and post-industrialism together produce are enduring. One day, diminishing returns might set in, as land costs and labour scarcities reduce the attractiveness of today's favoured places. But that can take a very long time to develop; meanwhile, generations live out their lives in areas contemplating nothing but decline. Left to global market forces and without imaginative local urban policy-making, a majority of towns and cities are being forced into economic and cultural mediocrity, if not poverty. Urban geographers have applied the concept of 'glocal' (drawn originally from Japanese agricultural policy) to express the way in which global pressures make it urgent for policy-makers to attend to what happens at the local level.[21]

It is not enough to provide generous social support for people who are unemployed or left in low-income occupations as a result of these processes, or to encourage firms and government organizations to locate back-office and warehouse activities in such places. We need collaboration among EU, national and local authorities to identify new activities that can thrive there – in particular, providing the infrastructure that will enable them to rival the already-favoured places, including iconic cultural projects, provided these reach into the daily lives of the population and are not just isolated pockets of elite activity fenced off from the rest of the city.[22] Also, as the German social scientist Marc Saxer has argued, maintaining a high-quality local environment of which people can be proud requires considerable public spending – a strategy that belongs to the left, not the populist right that claims to be the defender of *Heimat*, for whom it has a mainly cultural meaning.[23] Success in such a task will not be achieved everywhere; there will always be sad areas that fail to find a place in the changing world. But combinations of imaginative national and local planning with entrepreneurship, and determined attention to the geography of dynamism, can reduce their number, and therefore the numbers of those who feel left behind.

Subsidiarity also has a cultural dimension. A globalized world needs citizens who are at ease with a variety of layered identities – *matryoshka* dolls. But this means paying attention to the lower levels of little dolls as well as to the larger ones. We need to be able to feel loyalties and identities of varying strengths – to our local community, our town or city, our region, our country, our world region, our common humanity – that feed on and reinforce each other, not set in zero-sum conflict. The link between forward-looking economic development in the hands of local people able to be involved in the future of their cities and avoidance of a retreat into a world of warring tribes was identified by the US sociologist Benjamin Barber, who died in April 2017. He first set down these ideas in a book presciently entitled *Jihad versus McWorld: How Globalism and Tribalism are Reshaping the World* (published in 1995, six years before the massacre at the World Trade Center).[24]

Conclusion: pooled sovereignty and subsidiarity

Rodrik's most noted argument in *The Globalization Paradox* was his proposal that we today have a choice between democracy, national sovereignty and hyper-globalization, a trilemma. He argued that we could have any two of these, but not all three. 'Hyper-globalization' clearly implies the neoliberal ideal of totally unregulated globalization. Democracy separated from the nation state – the only form of democracy capable of dealing with the global economy – implies global democracy, which is impossible to achieve. A non-democratic nation state is compatible with hyper-globalization, because it implies a national 'sovereignty' willing to accept governance by the market and corporate power alone. This is a serious possibility. Analysing the messages of right-wing populist regimes in his native India, as well as Turkey, the USA, Russia, post-Brexit UK, Hungary and Poland, Arjun Appadurai identified three factors that these have in common: recognition that they cannot control their national economies; therefore, displacement of national identity onto cultural purification; and friendliness to neoliberal capitalism.[25]

In view of the priority that many observers rightly give to democracy, Rodrik's argument seems to lead to the conclusion that we can preserve democracy only by limiting political ambitions to the nation state and seeking to use it somehow to evade globalization. He has, therefore, become a key point of reference for left-wing opponents of Brexit in the UK, with nostalgia for the post-war Bretton Woods model of limited globalization without freedom of capital movements.

There is an alternative solution to Rodrik's trilemma. Globalization does not have to be 'hyper'. It can be moderated, through regulation by international agencies – which, although they cannot be fully democratic, can be subjected to democratic pressure, through the extension of democracy within world-regional economic associations, of which the EU is by far the leading example – and public debate over national policies within organizations like the OECD and WTO. Within such a framework, the nation state continues to play its role, both directly, in areas of autonomy where it remains capable of regulating globalization, and by democratizing its relationship to institutions of global governance. Nation states can decide – and it may well be rational for them to do so – to pool their sovereignty in order to extend its reach. This is a voluntary act, involving also a willingness to extend legitimacy to make decisions and to legislate, on behalf of the group of nation states so associated, to the organizations they construct. It assumes political will to achieve a social compromise across a number of countries based on recognition that: the high tide of neoliberal deregulation has been damaging; and national communities can only reassert regulation of that process by pooling their sovereignty and trying to introduce as much democracy as is practicable into that process. The trilemma becomes manageable. The gap between the three points of the Rodrik triangle is reduced when it is accepted that globalization requires some regulation, that the international agencies necessary to such regulation need elements of democracy, and that the democracy of the nation state best expresses itself as pooled sovereignty within that framework.

This approach then has to be combined with attention to local economic development and subsidiarity. Thus, the measures needed to regulate globalization have to move in two different directions, but this does not make them at all contradictory. First, there have to be moves towards pooled national sovereignty, partly through the construction, extension and democratization of world-regional entities like the European Union, and partly by developing in national debates strategies for using international organizations to improve the regulation of the global economy. There are few technical problems in designing appropriate policies; the difficulties are entirely those of political will. Second, and technically more difficult to achieve, ever more cities and regions must be able to develop dynamic economies that enable them to gain from globalization. This requires subsidiarity, with national and world-regional authorities helping such areas in their local policy-making tasks. As citizens, we need to respond to these challenges by becoming comfortable with multi-level identities and functioning politically in all of them.

There are some who intensely dislike the idea of multiple identities, favouring a jealous monopoly of important identity by one favoured level. Catalonian and Scottish separatists are examples, not content to express those identities within those of Spain and the UK – though, interestingly, the leading advocates of both are at ease with a European identity. The Spanish state is equally at odds with the requirements of modern citizenship with its attempts to take back from Catalonia and other regions the autonomy within Spain that they had enjoyed before. The British foreign secretary, Boris Johnson, has stated that in his view there is something worrying about people who see themselves as both British and European.[26] Referring specifically to young people who painted their faces with the EU flag, he wrote: 'I look at so many young people with the 12 stars lipsticked on their faces and I am troubled with the thought that people are beginning to have genuinely split allegiances.' Why must allegiances be seen as 'split' rather than as 'multiple'? Why the illiberal need for a state monopoly of identity?

In reality, many citizens are easily able to cope with multiple identities. For example, English football supporters will cheer to see the Belgian winger who plays for the Premier League team they support run rings round the English defender of the opposition team. But if exactly the same happens with the same players a week later when England are playing Belgium, their response will be one of despair. There is nothing contradictory about this; they simply know when to adopt one of their identities and when another. There is similarly no reason why people who aspire to transnational identities must be 'people of anywhere'. They may both be deeply rooted in their localities and love their country. The complexities of the modern world need them.

There is evidence from several countries that the monopolistically nationally minded are concentrated among older generations, and those at ease with multiple identities among the younger. The research of Oesch, Kitschelt and Rehm cited in chapter 3 suggests that professionals working at interpersonal tasks are more likely to combine liberal and egalitarian attitudes, and the automated economy of the future will see more people working in activities of that kind. There are counter-movements that abjure exclusive nationalism.[27] These straws in the wind give grounds for hope.

Notes

1 The Issues

1 W. Streeck, 2013. *Gekaufte Zeit. Die vertagte Krise des demokratischen Kapitalismus*. Berlin: Suhrkamp (translated in 2014 as *Buying Time*. London: Verso); 2015. 'The Rise of the European Consolidation State', MPIfG Discussion Paper 15/1. Cologne: Max Planck Institute for the Study of Societies; 2017. 'The Return of the Repressed as the Beginning of the End of Neoliberal Capitalism', in H. Geiselberger (ed.), *The Great Regression*. Cambridge: Polity (published originally as *Die große Regression*. Berlin: Suhrkamp), 157–72.
2 D. Goodhart, 2004. 'Too Diverse?' *Prospect*, February; 2013. *The British Dream: Successes and Failures of Post-War Immigration*. London: Atlantic.

2 The Economy

1 IMF, 2002. *Globalization: Threat or Opportunity?* Washington, DC: IMF.
2 F. Bourguignon, 2012. *La mondialisation de l'inégalité*.

Paris: Éditions de Seuil (translated in 2015 as *The Globalization of Inequality*. Princeton University Press).

3 B. Milanovic, 2016. *Global Inequality: a New Approach for the Age of Globalization*. Cambridge, MA: Harvard University Press.

4 D. Rodrik, 1997. *Has Globalization Gone Too Far?* Washington, DC: Peterson Institute for International Economics; 2011. *The Globalization Paradox: Democracy and the Future of the World Economy*. New York: W. W. Norton.

5 J. Stiglitz, 2002. *Globalization and its Discontents*. New York: W. W. Norton.

6 Readers wanting to learn more should consult J. Frieden, 2007. *Global Capitalism: Its Fall and Rise in the Twentieth Century*. New York: W. W. Norton.

7 L. Mosley, 2003. *Global Capital and National Governments*. Cambridge University Press; E. Rieger and S. Leibfried, 2001. *Grundlagen der Globalisierung*. Frankfurt am Main: Suhrkamp.

8 *The Guardian*, 27 June 2016.

9 https://data.worldbank.org/data-catalog/world-development-indicators.

10 https://www.wider.unu.edu/project/wiid-world-income-inequality-database. The Gini coefficient calculates the level of inequality of incomes in a country, where 1.00 represents a society in which all income is concentrated in the hands of one person, and 0.00 one with perfect income equality.

11 www.oecd-ilibrary.org/industry-and-services/iron-and-steel-industry-2005_iron_steel-2005-en-fr.

12 https://data.worldbank.org/indicator/SL.EMP.TOTL.SP.ZS?view=chart.

13 http://ec.europa.eu/eurostat/tgm/table.do?tab=table&init=1&language=en&pcode=t2020_10&plugin=1.

14 G. Standing, 2009. *Work after Globalization: Building*

Occupational Citizenship. Cheltenham: Edward Elgar; 2011. *The Precariat: The New Dangerous Class.* London: Bloomsbury.

15 A. L. Kalleberg, 2011. *Good Jobs, Bad Jobs.* New York: Russell Sage.

16 C. Crouch, 2015. *Governing Social Risks in Post-Crisis Europe.* Cheltenham: Edward Elgar.

17 OECD, 2018, https://stats.oecd.org/Index.aspx?DataSet Code=INVPT_I.

18 OECD, 2017, https://data.oecd.org/youthinac/youth-not-in-employment-education-or-training-neet.htm.

19 European Foundation for the Improvement of Living and Working Conditions, n.d. *Work-related Stress,* https://www.eurofound.europa.eu/sites/default/files/ef_files/docs/ewco/tn1004059s/tn1004059s.pdf.

20 F. Scharpf, 1991. *Crisis and Choice in European Social Democracy.* Ithaca, NY: Cornell University Press.

21 E. Moretti, 2016. *The New Geography of Jobs.* Boston, MA: Houghton Mifflin Harcourt; OECD, 2006. *Competitive Cities in the Global Economy,* OECD Territorial Reviews. Paris: OECD.

22 World Bank, 2001. *Global Economic Prospects and the Developing Countries 2001.* Washington, DC: World Bank.

23 Statistics Denmark, 2017. *Nordic Countries in Global Value Chains.* Copenhagen: Statistics Denmark.

24 OECD, 2017. 'Import Content of Exports', https://data.oecd.org/trade/import-content-of-exports.htm.

25 D. Cohen, 2017. 'Economic Sovereignty: a Delusion', *Social Europe,* 20 September, https://www.socialeurope.eu/economic-sovereignty-delusion.

26 An extended version of this example can be found in C. Crouch, 2017. 'Riddle: When Is a Chlorinated Chicken Better than a Regulated Banana?' *Social Europe,* 7 August, https://www.socialeurope.eu/riddle-chlorinated-chicken-better-regulated-banana.

3 Culture and Politics

1 See C. V. Wedgwood's classic study: 1957 [1938]. *The Thirty Years War*. London: Jonathan Cape.

2 S. Cotts Watkins, 1991. *From Provinces into Nations: Demographic Integration in Western Europe, 1870–1960*. Princeton University Press.

3 M. Oakeshott, 1962. 'On Being Conservative', in *Rationalism in Politics*. London: Methuen, 168–96.

4 D. Oesch, 2006. *Redrawing the Class Map*. Basingstoke: Palgrave Macmillan; 2006. 'Coming to Grips with a Changing Class Structure: an Analysis of Employment Stratification in Britain, Germany, Sweden and Switzerland', *International Sociology*, 21 (2), 263–88; D. Oesch and J. Rodríguez Menés, 2011. 'Upgrading or Polarization? Occupational Change in Britain, Germany, Spain and Switzerland, 1990–2008', *Socio-Economic Review*, 9 (3), 503–31.

5 H. Kitschelt and P. Rehm, 2014. 'Occupations as a Site of Political Preference Formation', *Comparative Political Studies*, 47 (12), 1670–1706.

6 E. Kaufmann, 2017. 'Trump and Brexit: Why it's again NOT the economy, stupid, LSE blog, http://blogs.lse. ac.uk/politicsandpolicy/trump-and-brexit-why-its-again-not-the-economy-stupid.

7 P. Mishra, 2017. *The Age of Anger*. London: Allen Lane.

8 M. Castells, 2017. *Ruptura. La crisis de la democracia liberal*. Madrid: Alianza Editorial.

9 Z. Bauman, 1999. *Liquid Modernity*. Cambridge: Polity.

10 B. Rothstein, 2017. 'Why Has the White Working Class Abandoned the Left?' *Social Europe*, 19 January, https:// www.socialeurope.eu/white-working-class-abandoned-left.

11 C. Crouch, 2004. *Post-Democracy*. Cambridge: Polity.

12 D. Goodhart, 2017. *The Road to Somewhere*. London: Hurst.
13 M. Duranti, 2017. *The Conservative Human Rights Revolution*. Oxford University Press.

4 The Future

1 D. della Porta and L. Mosca (eds.), 2003. *Globalizzazione e movimenti sociali*. Rome: Manifestolibri.
2 B. Mitchell and T. Fazi, 2017. *Reclaiming the State: a Progressive View of Sovereignty for a Post-Neoliberal World*. London: Pluto Press.
3 D. Goodhart, 2013. *The British Dream*. London: Atlantic.
4 Leviticus 19: 34.
5 F. W. Scharpf, 1999. *Governing in Europe*. Oxford University Press.
6 W. Streeck, 2013. *Gekaufte Zeit. Die vertagte Krise des demokratischen Kapitalismus*. Berlin: Suhrkamp (translated in 2014 as *Buying Time*. London: Verso).
7 M. Höpner, 2008. 'Usurpation statt Delegation: Wie der EuGH die Binnenmarktintegration radikalisiert und warum er politischer Kontrolle bedarf', MPIfG Discussion Paper 08/12. Cologne: MPIfG; 2014. 'Wie der Europäische Gerichtshof und die Kommission Liberalisierung durchsetzen', MPIfG Discussion Paper 14/8. Cologne: MPIfG.
8 P. de Grauwe and Y. Ji, 2016. 'Crisis Management and Economic Growth in the Eurozone', in F. Caselli (ed.), *Prospects for Growth in the European Union*. Oxford University Press.
9 IMF, 2015. 'The Effects of Structural Reform on Productivity', *World Economic Outlook*.
10 F. W. Scharpf, 2016. 'De-constitutionalization and Majority Rule', MPIfG Discussion Paper 16/14. Cologne: MPIfG.
11 For a prediction of these problems, made when the Euro

was first introduced, see the various contributions to C. Crouch (ed.), 2000. *After the Euro*. Oxford University Press.

12 D. Rodrik, 2016. 'Brexit and the Globalization Trilemma', http://rodrik.typepad.com/dani_rodriks_weblog/2016/06/brexit-and-the-globalization-trilemma.html; A. Evans-Pritchard, 2016. 'Brexit Vote is about the Sovereignty of Parliament and Nothing Else: Why I Am Voting to Leave the EU', *Daily Telegraph*, 13 June.

13 Y. Mounk, 2018. *The People versus Democracy*. Cambridge, MA: Harvard University Press.

14 W. I. Robinson, 2014. *Global Capitalism and the Crisis of Humanity*. Cambridge University Press.

15 Summarized by Hywel Ceri Jones, former EU director general for employment, social policy and industrial relations, in 'Free Movement and Migration: Labour's Challenge', *Social Europe*, 16 February 2018.

16 J. Stiglitz, 2002. *Globalization and its Discontents*. New York: W. W. Norton.

17 D. Rodrik, 1997. *Has Globalization Gone Too Far?* Washington, DC: Peterson Institute for International Economics.

18 D. Rodrik, 2011. *The Globalization Paradox: Democracy and the Future of the World Economy*. New York: W. W. Norton.

19 Heike Joebges, 2017. 'Crisis Recovery in a Country with a High Presence of Foreign Owned Companies: the Case of Ireland', IMK Working Paper 175. Düsseldorf: Hans Böckler Stiftung.

20 B. Harrington, 2017. *Capital without Borders*. Cambridge, MA: Harvard University Press.

21 For example, E. Swyngedouw and M. Kaika, 2003. 'The Making of "Glocal" Urban Modernities', *City*, 7 (1), 5–21.

22 For examples of such policies, see OECD, 2006.

Competitive *Cities in the Global Economy*, OECD Territorial Reviews. Paris: OECD.

23 M. Saxer, 2018. 'Linke Heimat', *IPG Journal,* 5 March, www.ipg-journal.de/schwerpunkt-des-monats/heimat/ artikel/detail/linke-heimat-2614.

24 B. Barber, 1995. *Jihad versus McWorld: How Globalism and Tribalism are Reshaping the World.* New York: Times Books.

25 A. Appadurai, 2017. 'Democracy Fatigue', in H. Geiselberger (ed.), *The Great Regression.* Cambridge: Polity (published originally as *Die große Regression.* Berlin: Suhrkamp), 1–12.

26 B. Johnson, 2017. 'My Vision for a Bold, Thrusting Britain Enabled by Brexit', *Daily Telegraph*, 15 September.

27 D. della Porta, 2017. 'Progressive and Regressive Politics in Late Neoliberalism', in H. Geiselberger (ed.), *The Great Regression*, 26–39.